CAMBRIDGE LIBRARY COLLECTION

Books of enduring scholarly value

British and Irish History, Seventeenth and Eighteenth Centuries

The books in this series focus on the British Isles in the early modern period, as interpreted by eighteenth- and nineteenth-century historians, and show the shift to 'scientific' historiography. Several of them are devoted exclusively to the history of Ireland, while others cover topics including economic history, foreign and colonial policy, agriculture and the industrial revolution. There are also works in political thought and social theory, which address subjects such as human rights, the role of women, and criminal justice.

An Essay on the First Principles of Government

In this 1768 publication, Joseph Priestley (1733–1804) expounds his political philosophy, revealed in part through his earlier writings on education and theology. While teaching at the dissenting academy at Warrington, he had argued against a scheme of national education in his *Essay on a Course of Liberal Education* (1765), included and expanded on in his *Miscellaneous Observations Relating to Education* (1778), which has been reissued in this series. Here, he explains that freedoms of education and religion promote free discourse, which is essential for social progress. Such discourse is only possible when government protects both civil liberty, power over one's own actions, and political liberty, the right to vote and hold office. Although harshly criticised at first for its perceived attack on church and government authority, Priestley's work inspired later liberal political theorists, notably enthusing Jeremy Bentham with its incorporation of a principle of utility.

T0370908

Cambridge University Press has long been a pioneer in the reissuing of out-of-print titles from its own backlist, producing digital reprints of books that are still sought after by scholars and students but could not be reprinted economically using traditional technology. The Cambridge Library Collection extends this activity to a wider range of books which are still of importance to researchers and professionals, either for the source material they contain, or as landmarks in the history of their academic discipline.

Drawing from the world-renowned collections in the Cambridge University Library and other partner libraries, and guided by the advice of experts in each subject area, Cambridge University Press is using state-of-the-art scanning machines in its own Printing House to capture the content of each book selected for inclusion. The files are processed to give a consistently clear, crisp image, and the books finished to the high quality standard for which the Press is recognised around the world. The latest print-on-demand technology ensures that the books will remain available indefinitely, and that orders for single or multiple copies can quickly be supplied.

The Cambridge Library Collection brings back to life books of enduring scholarly value (including out-of-copyright works originally issued by other publishers) across a wide range of disciplines in the humanities and social sciences and in science and technology.

An Essay on
the First Principles
of Government

And on the Nature of Political,
Civil, and Religious Liberty

JOSEPH PRIESTLEY

CAMBRIDGE
UNIVERSITY PRESS

University Printing House, Cambridge, CB2 8BS, United Kingdom

Published in the United States of America by Cambridge University Press, New York

Cambridge University Press is part of the University of Cambridge.
It furthers the University's mission by disseminating knowledge in the pursuit of
education, learning and research at the highest international levels of excellence.

www.cambridge.org
Information on this title: www.cambridge.org/9781108064866

© in this compilation Cambridge University Press 2013

This edition first published 1768
This digitally printed version 2013

ISBN 978-1-108-06486-6 Paperback

A N

E S S A Y

ON THE

FIRST PRINCIPLES

OF

GOVERNMENT;

AND ON THE NATURE OF

Political, Civil, and Religious

L I B E R T Y.

By JOSEPH PRIESTLEY, LL.D. F.R.S.

LONDON:

Printed for J. Dodsley, in Pall-Mall; T. Cadell (fuc-
ceffor to Mr. Millar) in the Strand; and J. Johnson,
Nº. 8, Pafter-nofter Row.

MDCCLXVIII.

T H E

P R E F A C E.

THIS publication owes its rife to the *remarks* I formerly wrote *on Dr. Brown's propofal for a code of education*. Several perfons who were pleafed to think favourably of that performance, (in which I was led to mention the fubject of civil and religious liberty) were defirous that I fhould treat of it more at large, and without any immediate view to the doctor's work. It appeared to them, that fome of the views I had given of this important, but difficult fubject, were new, and fhowed it, in a clearer light than any in which they had feen it reprefented before. They thought I had placed the foundation of thofe moft valuable interefts of mankind on a broader and firmer bafis, in confequence of my availing myfelf of a more accurate and ex-

A   tenfive

tenfive fyftem of morals and policy, than was adopted by Mr. Locke, and others who formerly wrote upon this fubject. I have endeavoured to anfwer the wifhes of my friends, in the beft manner I am able; and, at the fame time, I have retained the fubftance of the former treatife, having diftributed the feveral parts of it into the body of this.

Let it be obferved however, that, in this treatife, I propofe no more than to confider *the firft principles* of civil and religious liberty, and to explain fome leading ideas upon the fubject. For a more extenfive view of it, as affecting a greater variety of particulars in the fyftem of government, I refer to *the courfe of lectures on hiftory and civil policy*; a *fyllabus* of which is printed in the *Effay on a courfe of liberal education for civil and active life*, and the whole of which, with enlargements, I propofe to publifh in due time. I make no apology for the *freedom* with which I have written. The
fub-

fubject is, in the higheft degree, interefting to humanity, it is open to philofophical difcuffion, and I have taken no greater liberties than becomes a philofopher, a man, and an Englifhman. Having no other views than to promote a thorough knowledge of this important fubject, not being fenfible of any biafs to miflead me in my inquiries, and confcious of the uprightnefs of my intentions, I freely fubmit my thoughts to the examination of all impartial judges, and the friends of their country and of mankind. They who know the fervour of generous feelings will be fenfible, that I have expreffed myfelf with no more warmth than the importance of the fubject neceffarily prompted, in a breaft not naturally the coldeft; and that to have appeared more indifferent, I could not have been fincere.

It will be a great miftake to imagine, that, in this treatife, I fpeak the language of *any party*.　I only give my own ideas of things, without the concurrence of any

perfon

perfon whatever; fo that if any thing in them be wrong, myfelf only am anfwerable for it.

Notwithftanding the ardour of mind with which, it will be evident, fome parts of the following treatife were written, the warmth with which I have efpoufed the caufe of liberty, and the feverity with which I have animadverted upon whatever I apprehend to be unfavourable to it; I think I cannot be juftly accufed of party zeal, becaufe it will be found, that I have treated all parties with equal freedom.   Indeed, fuch is the ufual violence of human paffions, when any thing interefting to them is contended for, that the beft caufe in the world is not fufficient to prevent intemperance and excefs; fo that it is eafy to fee too much to blame in all parties : and it by no means follows, that, becaufe a man difapproves of the conduct of one, that he muft, therefore, approve of that of its oppofite.   The greateft enemy of

popery

popery may fee fomething he diflikes in the conduct of the firft reformers, the warmeft zeal againft epifcopacy is confiftent with a juft fenfe of the faults of the puritans, and much more may an enemy of Charles the firft, be an enemy of Cromwell alfo.

THE

THE

CONTENTS.

THE

INTRODUCTION.

Of the First Principles of Government, and the Nature of Liberty.

MAN derives two capital advantages from the superiority of his intellectual powers.

The first is, that, as an individual, he possesses a certain comprehension of mind, whereby he contemplates and enjoys the past and the future, as well as the present. By this means his happiness is less dependent on temporary circumstances and sensations. Ideas collected from a certain limited space, on each side of the present moment, are always

B   ready

ready to crowd upon his mind, and to temper, and exalt his feelings.

This fpace, which is the fphere of a man's comprehenfion, of which he has the enjoyment, and which may be called the extent of his *prefent time*, is greater or lefs, in proportion to the progrefs he has made in intellect, and his advancement above mere animal nature ; and it is generally growing larger during the whole courfe of our lives. A child is fenfible of nothing beyond the prefent moment, being little more than a brute animal ; though the actual feelings of perfons advanced in life never depend wholly upon the prefent moment, but are greatly influenced both by the remembrance of what is paft, and the expectation of what is future.

Thefe intellectual pleafures and pains, in many cafes, wholly over power all temporary fenfations; whereby fome men, of great and fuperior minds, enjoy a
ftate

ftate of permanent and equable felicity, in a great meafure independent of the uncertain accidents of life. In fuch minds the ideas of things, that are feen to be the caufe and effect of one another, perfectly coalefce into one, and prefent but one common image. Thus all the ideas of evil abfolutely vanifh, in the idea of the greater good with which it is connected, or of which it is productive.

To this comprehenfion of mind, which is extending with the experience of every day, no bounds can be fet. Nay, it fhould feem, that while our faculties of perception and action remain in the fame vigour, our progrefs towards perfection muft be continually accelerated; and that nothing but a future exiftence, in advantageous circumftances, is requifite to advance a mere man above every thing we can now conceive of excellence and perfection. This train of thought may, in fome meafure, enable us to conceive

B 2   wherein

wherein confifts the fuperiority of angelic beings, whofe fphere of comprehenfion, that is, whofe *prefent time*, may be of proportionably greater extent than ours, owing to the greater extent of their recollection and forefight; and even give us fome faint idea of the incomprehenfible excellence and happinefs of the Divine Being, in whofe view nothing is paft or future, but to whom the whole compafs of duration is, to every real purpofe, without diftinction prefent.

> " Who fills his own eternal NOW,
> " And fees our ages wafte."
>
> WATTS.

The next advantage refulting from the fame principle, and which is, in many refpects, both the caufe and effect of the former, is, that the human fpecies itfelf is capable of a fimilar and unbounded improvement ; whereby mankind in a later age are greatly fuperior

to

to mankind in a former age, the individuals being taken at the fame time of
life. Of this progrefs of the fpecies,
brute animals are more incapable than
they are of that relating to individuals.
No horfe of this age feems to have any
advantage over the individuals of this
kind that lived many centuries ago;
and if there be any improvement in the
fpecies, it is owing to our manner of
breeding and training them. But a man
at this time, who has been tolerably well
educated, in an improved chriftian country, is a being poffeffed of much greater
power, to be, and to make happy, than
a perfon of the fame age, in the fame, or
any other country, fome centuries ago.
And, for this reafon, I make no doubt,
that a perfon fome centuries hence will,
at the fame age, be as much fuperior
to us.

The great inftrument in the hand
of divine providence, of this progrefs
of the fpecies towards perfection, is *fo-*

B 3   *ciety,*

ciety, and confequently *government.* In a ftate of nature the powers of a fingle man are diffipated by an attention to a multiplicity of objects. The employments of all are fimilar. From generation to generation every man does the fame that every other does, or has done; and no perfon begins where another ends; at leaft, general improvements are exceeding flow, and uncertain. This we fee exemplified in all barbarous nations, and efpecially in countries thinly inhabited, where the connections of the people are flight, and confequently fociety and government very imperfect; and it may be feen more particularly in North America, and Greenland. Whereas a ftate of more perfect fociety admits of a proper diftribution and divifion of the objects of human attention. In fuch a ftate, men are connected with and fubfervient to one another; fo that, while one man confines himfelf to one fingle object, another may give the fame undivided attention to another object.

Thus

Thus the powers of all have their full effect: and hence arife improvements in all the conveniences of life, and in every branch of knowledge. In this ftate of things, it requires but a few years to comprehend the whole preceding pro-grefs of any one art or fcience; and the reft of a man's life, in which his facul-ties are the moft perfect, may be given to the extenfion of it. If, by this means, one art or fcience fhould grow too large for an eafy comprehenfion in a moderate fpace of time, a commodious fubdivifion will be made. Thus all knowledge will be fubdivided and extended; and *know-ledge*, as Lord *Bacon* obferves, being *power*, the human powers will, in fact, be increafed; nature, including both its materials, and its laws, will be more at our command; men will make their fitua-tion in this world abundantly more eafy and comfortable; they will probably prolong their exiftence in it, and will grow daily more happy, each in himfelf, and more able (and, I believe, more dif-

B 4   pofed)

pofed) to communicate happinefs to others. Thus, whatever was the beginning of this world, the end will be glorious and paradifaical, beyond what our imagiations can now conceive. Extravagant as fome may fuppofe thefe views to be, I think I could fhow them to be fairly fuggefted by the true theory of human nature, and to arife from the natural courfe of human affairs. But, for the prefent, I wave this fubject, the contemplation of which always makes me happy.

Government being the great inftrument of this progrefs of the human fpecies towards this glorious ftate, that form of government will have a juft claim to our approbation which favours this progrefs, and that muft be condemned in which it is retarded. Let us then, my fellow citizens, confider the bufinefs of government with thefe enlarged views, and trace fome of the fundamental principles of it, by an attention to what is moft conducive

to

to the happinefs of mankind at prefent, and moft favourable to the increafe of this happinefs in futurity; and, perhaps, we may underftand this intricate fubject, with fome of its moft important circumftances, better than we have done; at leaft we may fee fome of them in a clearer and ftronger point of light.

To begin with firft principles, we muft, for the fake of gaining clear ideas on the fubject, do what almoft all political writers have done before us; that is, we muft fuppofe a number of people exifting, who experience the inconvenience of living independent and unconnected; who are expofed, without redrefs, to infults and wrongs of every kind; and too weak to procure themfelves many of the advantages, which they are fenfible might eafily be compaffed by united ftrength. Thefe people, if they would engage the protection of the whole body, and join their force in enterprizes and undertakings calculated for their common good,

muft

muſt voluntarily reſign ſome part of their natural liberty, and ſubmit their conduct to the direction of the community : for without theſe conceſſions, ſuch an alliance, attended with ſuch advantages, could not be formed.

Were theſe people few in number, and living within a ſmall diſtance of one another, it might be eaſy for them to aſſemble upon every occaſion, in which the whole body was concerned ; and every thing might be determined by the votes of the majority, provided they had previouſly agreed that the votes of a majority ſhould be deciſive. But were the ſociety numerous, their habitations remote, and the occaſions in which the whole body muſt interpoſe frequent, it would be abſolutely impoſſible that all the members of the ſtate ſhould aſſemble, or give their attention to public buſineſs. In this caſe, whether, with *Rouſſeau,* it be a giving up of their liberty or not, there muſt be deputies, or public officers, appointed to act

in

in the name of the whole body; and, in
a ſtate of very great extent, where all
the people could never be aſſembled, the
whole power of the community muſt
neceſſarily, and almoſt irreverſibly, be
lodged in the hands of theſe deputies.
In England, the king, the hereditary
lords, and the electors of the houſe of
commons, are theſe *ſtanding* deputies; and
the members of the houſe of commons
are, again, the *temporary* deputies of this
laſt order of the ſtate.

In all ſtates, great or ſmall, the ſentiments of that body of men in whoſe
hands the ſupreme power of the ſociety is
lodged, muſt be underſtood to be the
ſentiments of the whole body, if there
be no other method in which the ſentiments of the whole body can be ex-
preſſed. Theſe deputies, or repreſentatives of the people, will make a wrong
judgment, and purſue wrong meaſures, if
they conſult not the good of the whole
ſociety, whoſe repreſentatives they are;
juſt

juſt as the people themſelves would make a wrong judgment, and purſue wrong meaſures, if they did not conſult their own good, provided they could be aſſembled for that purpoſe; but, like the people, in whoſe place they ſtand, no power on earth has a right to control their judgments. No maxims or rules of policy can be binding upon them, but ſuch as they themſelves ſhall judge to be conducive to the public good. Their own reaſon and conſcience are their only guide, and the people, in whoſe name they act, their only judge.

In theſe circumſtances, if I be asked what I mean by *liberty*, I ſhould chuſe, for the ſake of greater clearneſs, to divide it into two kinds, *political*, and *civil*; and the importance of having clear ideas on this ſubject will be my apology for the innovation. *Political liberty*, I would ſay, conſiſts in the power, which the members of the ſtate reſerve to themſelves, of arriving at the public offices, or at leaſt of
having

having votes in the nomination of thofe who fill them : and I would chufe to call *civil liberty* that power over their own actions, which the members of the ftate referve to themfelves, and which their officers muft not infringe. Political liberty, therefore, is equivalent to the right of magiftracy, being the claim that any member of the ftate hath, to have his private opinion or judgment become that of the public, and thereby control the actions of others; whereas civil liberty, extends no farther than to a man's own conduct, and fignifies the right he has to be exempt from the control of the fociety, or its agents ; that is, the power he has of providing for his own advantage and happinefs. It is a man's civil liberty, which is originally in its full force, and part of which he facrifices when he enters into a ftate of fociety; and political liberty is that which he may or may not acquire in the compenfation he receives for it. For he may either ftipulate to have a voice in the public determinations, or, as far as the public determination

termination dothtake place, he may fubmit to be governed wholly by others. Of
thefe two kinds of liberty, which it is of
the greateft importance to diftinguifh, I
fhall treat in the order in which I have
mentioned them.

PART

PART I.

OF

POLITICAL LIBERTY.

IN countries where every member of the fociety enjoys an equal power of arriving at the fupreme offices, and confequently of directing the ftrength and the fentiments of the whole community, there is a ftate of the moft perfect political liberty. On the other hand, in countries where a man is, by his birth or fortune, excluded from thefe offices, or from a power of voting for proper perfons to fill them; that man, whatever be the form of the government, or whatever civil liberty, or power over his own actions he may have,

have, has no power over thofe of another, has no fhare in the government, and therefore has no political liberty at all. Nay his own conduct, as far as the fociety does interfere, is, in all cafes, directed by others.

It may be faid, that no fociety on earth was ever formed in the manner reprefented above. I anfwer, it is true; becaufe all governments whatever have been, in fome meafure, compulfory, tyrannical, and oppreffive in their origin; but the method I have defcribed muft be allowed to be the only equitable and fair method of forming a fociety. And fince every man retains, and can never be deprived of his natural right (founded on a regard to the general good) of relieving himfelf from all oppreffion, that is, from every thing that has been impofed upon him without his own confent; this can be the only true and proper foundation of all the governments fubfifting in the world, and that to which the people who com-

pofe

pofe them have an unalienable right to bring them back.

It muft neceffarily be underftood, therefore, whether it be expreffed or not, that all people live in fociety for their mutual advantage; fo that the good and happinefs of the members, that is the majority of the members of any ftate, is the great ftandard by which every thing relating to that ftate muft finally be determined. And though it may be fuppofed, that a body of people may be bound by a voluntary refigna-tion of all their interefts (which they have been fo infatuated as to make) to a fingle perfon, or to a few, it can never be fuppofed that the refignation is obli-gatory to their pofterity; becaufe it is manifeftly *contrary to the good of the whole that it fhould be fo.*

I own it is rather matter of furprife to me, that this great objeft of all go-vernment fhould have been fo little in-

fifted

fisted on by our great writers who have treated of this subject, and that more use hath not been made of it. In treating of particular regulations in states, this principle necessarily obtruded itself; all arguments in favour of any law being always drawn from a consideration of its tendency to promote the public good; and yet it has often escaped the notice of writers in discoursing on the first principles of society, and the subject of civil and religious liberty.

This one general idea, properly pursued, throws the greatest light upon the whole system of policy, morals, and, I may add, theology too. To a mind not warped by theological and metaphysical subtilties, the divine being appears to be actuated by no other views than the noblest we can conceive, the happiness of his creatures. Virtue and right conduct consist in those affections and actions which terminate in the public good; justice and veracity, for instance,

ftance, having nothing intrinfically excellent in them, feparate from their relation to the happinefs of mankind ; and
the whole fyftem of right to power,
property, and every thing elfe in fociety,
muft be regulated by the fame confideration : the decifive queftion, when any
of thefe fubjects are examined being ; what
is it that the good of the community
requires ?

Let it be obferved, in this place, that
I by no means affert, that the good of
mankind requires a ftate of the moft perfect political liberty. This, indeed, is
not poffible, except in exceeding fmall
ftates ; in none, perhaps, that are fo
large as even the republics of ancient
Greece ; or as Genoa, or Geneva in
modern times. Such fmall republics as
thefe, if we judge from experience, are
not defirable ; becaufe not favourable to
great improvements and to happinefs. If
they were defirable, they would be
impracticable ; becaufe a ftate of perfect equality, in communities or individuals,

viduals, can never be preferved, while fome are more powerful, more enterprifing, and more fuccefsful in their attempts than others. And an ambitious nation could not wifh for a fairer opportunity of arriving at extenfive empire, than finding the neighbouring countries cantoned out into a number of fmall governments, which could have no power to withftand it fingly, and which could never form fufficiently extenfive confederacies, or act with fufficient unanimity, and expedition, to oppofe it with fuccefs. Suppofing, therefore, that in order to prevent the greateft of all inconveniences, very extenfive, and conquently abfolute monarchies, it may be expedient to have fuch ftates as England, France, and Spain; even here political liberty muft, in fome meafure, be reftrained; but in what manner a reftraint fhould be put upon it, and how far it fhould extend, is not eafy to be afcertained. In general, it fhould feem, that none but perfons of confiderable fortune fhould be capable of arriving at the higheft offices in

the

the government; not only becaufe, all
other circumftances being equal, fuch perfons will generally have had the beft education, and confequently be the beft
qualified to act for the public good; but
alfo, as they will neceffarily have the moft
property at ftake, and will, therefore,
be moft interefted in the fate of their
country.

For the fame reafon, it may, perhaps,
be more eligible, that thofe who are extremely dependent fhould not be allowed to have votes in the nomination of
the chief magiftrates; becaufe this might
in fome inftances, be only throwing
more votes into the hands of thofe perfons on whom they depend. But if, in
every ftate of confiderable extent, we
fuppofe a gradation of elective offices, and if we likewife fuppofe the
loweft claffes of the people to have votes
in the nomination of the loweft officers,
and, as they increafe in wealth and importance, to have a fhare in the choice of

C 3   per-

perſons to fill the higher poſts, till they themſelves be admitted candidates for places of public truſt ; we ſhall, perhaps, form an idea of as much political liberty as is conſiſtent with the ſtate of mankind. And I think experience ſhews, that the higheſt offices of all, equivalent to that of king, ought to be in ſome meaſure hereditary, as in England ; elective monarchies having generally been the theatre of cabals, confuſion, and miſery.

But though the exact medium of political liberty be not eaſily fixed, it is not of much conſequence to do it ; ſince a conſiderable degree of perfection in government will admit of great varieties in this reſpect ; and the extreme of political ſlavery, which excludes all perſons, except one, or a very few, from having acceſs to the chief magiſtracy, or from having votes in the choice of magiſtrates, is eaſily marked out, and the fatal effects of it are very ſtriking. For ſuch is the
ſtate

ftate of mankind, that perfons poffeffed of unbounded power will generally act as if they forgot the proper nature and defign of their ftation, and purfue their own intereft, though it be oppofite to that of the community at large.

But if there be any truth in the principles above laid down, it muft be a fundamental maxim in all governments, that if any man hold what is called a high rank, or enjoy privileges, and prerogatives in a ftate, it is becaufe the good of the ftate requires that he fhould hold that rank, or enjoy thofe privileges; and fuch perfons, whether they be called kings, fenators, or nobles; or by whatever names, or titles, they be diftinguifhed, are, to all intents and purpofes, the fervants of the public, and accountable to the people for the difcharge of their refpective offices.

If fuch magiftrates abufe their truft, in the people, therefore, lies the right

of

of depofing, and confequently of punifhing them. And the only reafon why
abufes which have crept into offices
have been connived at, is, that the cor-
recting of them, by having recourfe to
firft principles, and the people taking
into their own hands their right to
appoint or change their officers, and to
afcertain the bounds of their authority, is far from being eafy, except in
fmall ftates; fo that the remedy would
often be worfe than the difeafe.

But, in the largeft ftates, if the a-
bufes of government fhould, at any time,
be great and manifeft; if the fervants
of the people, forgetting their mafters,
and their mafter's intereft, fhould purfue
a feparate one of their own; if, inftead
of confidering that they are made for the
people, they fhould confider the people as made for them; if the oppreffions and violations of right fhould be
great, flagrant, and univerfally refented;
if the tyranical governors fhould have

no

no friends but a few fycophants, who had long preyed upon the vitals of their fellow citizens, and who might be expected to defert a government, whenever their interefts fhould be detached from it: if, in confequence of thefe circumftances, it fhould become manifeft, that the rifque, which would be run in attempting a revolution would be trifling, and the evils which might be apprehended from it, were far lefs than thefe which were actually fuffered, and which were daily increafing; in the name of God, I afk, what principles are thofe, which ought to reftrain an injured and infulted people from afferting their natural rights, and from changing, or even punifhing their governors, that is their fervants, who had abufed their truft; or from altering the whole form of their government, if it appeared to be of a ftructure fo liable to abufe?

To fay that thefe forms of government

ment have been long eftablifhed, and that thefe oppreffions have been long fuffered, without any complaint, is to fupply the ftrongeft argument for their abolition. Lawyers, who are governed by rules and precedents, are very apt to fall into miftakes, in determining what is right and lawful, in cafes which are, in their own nature, prior to any fixed laws or precedents. The only reafon for the authority of precedents and general rules in matters of law and government, is, that all perfons may know what is law; which they could not do if the adminiftration of it was not uniform, and the fame in fimilar cafes. But if the precedents and general rules themfelves be a greater grievance than the violation of them, and the eftablifhment of better precedents, and better general rules, what becomes of their obligation? The neceffity of the thing, in the changing courfe of human affairs, obliges all governments to alter their general rules, and to fet up new precedent dents in affairs of lefs importance; and why may not a proportionably greater neceffity plead as ftrongly for the alteration of the moft general rules, and for fetting up new precedents in matters of the greateft confequence, affecting the moft fundamental principles of any government, and the diftribution of power among its feveral members?

Nothing can more juftly excite the indignation of an honeft and oppreffed citizen, than to hear a prelate, who enjoys a confiderable benefice, under a corrupt government, pleading for its fupport by thofe abominable perverfions of fcripture, which have been too common on this occafion; as by urging in its favour that paffage of St. Paul, *The powers which be are ordained of God,* and others of a fimilar import. It is a fufficient anfwer to fuch an abfurd quotation as this, that, for the fame reafon, the powers which *will be* will be ordained of God alfo.

Some-

Something, indeed, might have been said in favour of the doctrines of paffive obedience and non-refiftance, at the time when they were firft ftarted; but a man muft be infatuated who will not renounce them now. The Jefuits, about two centuries ago, in order to vindicate their king-killing principles, happened, among other arguments, to make ufe of this great and juft principle, that all civil power is ultimately derived from the people: and their adverfaries, in England, and elfewhere, inftead of fhewing how they abufed and perverted that fundamental principle of all government in the cafe in queftion, did, what difputants warmed with controverfy are very apt to do; they denied the principle itfelf, and maintained that all civil power is derived from God, as if the Jewifh theocracy had been eftablifhed throughout the whole world. From this maxim it was a clear confequence, that the governments, which at any time fubfift, being the ordinance of God, and the kings which are at any time

time upon the throne, being the vicege-
rents of God, muft not be oppofed.

So long as there were recent examples
of good kings depofed, and fome of them
maffacred by wild enthufiafts, fome indulgence might be allowed to thofe
warm, but weak friends of fociety, who
would lay hold of any principle, which,
however ill founded, would fupply an argument for more effectually preferving
the publick peace ; but to maintain the
fame abfurd principles at this day, when
the danger from which they ferved to
fhelter us is over, and the heat of controverfy is abated, fhews the ftrongeft and
moft blameable prepoffeffion. Writers
in defence of them do not deferve a ferious anfwer: and to alledge thofe principles in favour of a corrupt government,
which nothing can excufe but their being
brought in favour of a good one, is un-
pardonable.

The

The hiftory of this controverfy about the doctrine of paffive obedience and non-refiftance, affords a ftriking example of the danger of having recourfe to falfe principles in controverfy. They may ferve a particular turn, but, in other cafes, may be capable of the moft dangerous application; whereas univerfal truth will, in all poffible cafes, have the beft confequences, and be ever favourable to the true interefts of mankind.

It will be faid, that it is opening a door to rebellion, to affert that magiftrates, abufing their power, may be fet afide by the people, who are of courfe their own judges when that power is abufed. May not the people, it is faid, abufe their power, as well as their governors? I anfwer, it is very poffible they may abufe their power: it is poffible they may imagine themfelves oppreffed when they are not: it is poffible that their animofity may be artfully and unreafonably inflamed, by ambitious and enterprifing men,

men, whofe views are often beft anfwered by popular tumults and infurrections; and the people may fuffer in confequence of their folly and precipitancy. But what man is there, or what body of men (whofe right to direct their own conduct was never called in queftion) but are liable to be impofed upon, and to fuffer in confequence of their miftaken apprehenfions and precipitate conduct?

With refpect to large focieties, it is very improbable, that the people fhould be too foon alarmed, fo as to be driven to thefe extremities. In fuch cafes, the power of the government, that is, of the governors, muft be very extenfive and arbitrary; and the power of the people fcattered, and difficult to be united; fo that, if a man have common fenfe, he will fee it to be madnefs to propofe, or to lay any meafure for a general infurrection againft the government, except in cafe of very general and great oppreffion. Even patriots, in fuch circumftances,

will

will confider, that prefent evils always appear greater in confequence of their being prefent ; but that the future evils of a revolt, and a temporary anarchy, may be much greater than are apprehended at a diftance. They will, alfo, confider, that unlefs their meafures be perfectly well laid, and their fuccefs decifive, ending in a change, not of men, but of things; not of governors, but of the rules and adminiftration of government, they will only rivet their chains the fafter, and bring upon themfelves and their country tenfold ruin.

The cafe, I own, may be otherwife in lefs extenfive ftates, where the power of the governors is comparatively fmall, and the power of the people great, and foon united. Thefe fears, therefore, may be prudent in Venice, in Genoa, or in the fmall cantons of Switzerland; but it were to the laft degree, abfurd to extend them to Great-Britain.

T h

The Englifh hiftory will inform us, that the people of this country have always borne extreme oppreffion, for a long time before there has appeared any danger of a general infurrection againft the government. What a feries of encroachments upon their rights did even the feudal barons, whofe number was very confiderable, and whofe power was great, bear from William the Conqueror, and his fucceffors, before they broke out into actual rebellion on that account, as in the reigns of king John, and Henry the third ! And how much were the loweft orders of the poor commons trampled upon with impunity by both, till a much later period ; when, all the while, they were fo far from attempting any refiftance, or even complaining of the grofs infringements of their rights, that they had not fo much as the idea of their having any rights to be trampled upon ! After the people had begun to acquire property, independance, and an idea of their natural rights, how long did

D   they

they bear a load of old and new oppreffions under the Tudors, but more efpecially under the Stuarts, before they
broke out into what the friends of arbitrary power affect to call *the grand rebellion!* And how great did that obftinate civil war fhow the power of the
king to be, notwithftanding the moft
intolerable and wanton abufe of it! At
the clofe of the year 1642, it was more
probable that the king would have pre-
vailed than the parliament; and his fuccefs would have been certain, if his conduct had not been as weak, as it was
wicked.

So great was the power of the crown,
that, after the reftoration, Charles the
fecond was tempted to act the fame part
with his father, and actually did it, in a
great meafure, with impunity; till, at
laft, he was even able to reign without
parliaments; and if he had lived much
longer, he would, in all probability, have
been as arbitrary as the king of France.

His

His brother James the fecond, had almoft fubverted both the civil and religious liberties of his country, in the
fhort fpace of four years, and might
have done it completely, if he could
have been content to have proceeded
with more caution; nay, he might have
fucceeded notwithftanding his precipitancy, if the divine being had not, at
that critical time, raifed up William the
third of glorious memory, for our deli-
verance. But, God be thanked, the government of this country is now fixed
upon fo good and firm a bafis, and is fo
generally aquiefced in, that they are
only the mere tools of a court party, or
the narrow minded bigots among the
inferior clergy, who, to ferve their
own low purpofes, do now and then
promote the cry, that the church or the
ftate is in danger.

As to what is called the crime of *rebellion*, we have nothing to do either
with the name, or the thing, in the cafe
before

before us. That term, if it admit of any definition, is an attempt to fubvert a lawful government; but the queftion is, whether an oppreffive government, though it have been ever fo long eftablifhed, can be a lawful one; or, to cut off all difpute about words, if lawful, legal, and conftitutional, be maintained to be the fame thing, whether the lawful, legal, and conftitutional government be a *good* government, or one in which fufficient provifion is made for the happinefs of the fubjects of it. If it fail in this effential character, refpecting the true end and object of all civil government, no other property or title, with which it may be dignified, ought to fhelter it from the generous attack of the noble and daring patriot. If the bold attempt be precipitate, and unfuccefsful, the tyrannical government will be fure to term it rebellion, but that cenfure cannot make the thing itfelf lefs glorious. The memory of fuch brave, though unfuccefsful and unfortunate friends of liberty,

berty, and of the rights of mankind, as
that of Harmodius and Ariftogiton
among the Athenians, and Ruffel and
Sidney in our own country, will be
had in everlafting honour by their grateful fellow citizens; and hiftory will fpeak
another language than laws.

If it be afked how far a people may
lawfully go in punifhing their chief
magiftrates, I anfwer that, if the enor-
mity of the offence (which is of the fame
extent as the injury done to the public)
be confidered, any punifhment is jufti-
fiable that a man can incur in human fociety. It may be faid, there are no
laws to punifh thofe governors, and we
muft not condemn perfons by laws made
ex poft facto; for this conduct will vindicate the moft obnoxious meafures of the
moft tyrannical adminiftration. But I
anfwer, that this is a cafe, in its own nature, prior to the eftablifhment of any
laws whatever; as it affects the very
being of fociety, and defeats the prin-

D 3   cipal

cipal ends for which recourfe was originally had to it. There may be no fixed
law againſt an open invader who ſhould
attempt to ſeize upon a country, with a
view to enſlave all its inhabitants ; but
muſt not the invader be apprehended, and
even put to death, though he have broken
no expreſs law then in being, or none
of which he was properly apprized ?
And why ſhould a man, who takes the
advantage of his being king, or gover-
nor, to ſubvert the laws and liberties of
his country, be confidered in any other
light than that of a foreign invader ?
Nay his crime is much more atrocious,
as he was appointed the guardian of the
laws and liberties, which he ſubverts,
and therefore was under the ſtrongeſt
obligation to maintain.

In a caſe, therefore, of this highly
criminal nature, *ſalus populi ſuprema eſt
lex.* That muſt be done which the good
of the whole requires ; and, generally,
kings depoſed, baniſhed, or impriſoned,
are

are highly dangerous to a nation; be-
cause, let them have governed ever fo ill,
it will be the intereft of fome to be
their partifans, and to attach themfelves
to their caufe.

It will be fuppofed, that thefe obfervations have a reference to what paffed
in England in the year 1648. Let it be
fuppofed. Surely a man, and an Englifhman, may be at liberty to give his
opinion, freely and without difguife, concerning a tranfaction of fo old a date.
Charles the firft, whatever he was in his
private character, which is out of the
queftion here, was certainly a very bad
king of England. During a courfe of
many years, and notwithftanding repeated remonftrances, he governed by
maxims utterly fubverfive of the fundamental and free conftitution of this
country; and, therefore, he deferved
the fevereft punifhment. If he was
mifled by his education, or his friends,

he

he was, like any other criminal, in the fame circumftances, to be pitied, but by no means to be fpared on that account.

From the nature of things it was neceffary that the oppofition fhould begin from a few, who may, therefore, be ftiled a *faction*; but after the civil war (which neceffarily enfued from the king's obftinacy, and in which he had given repeated inftances of diffimulation and treachery) there was evidently no fafety, either for the faction or the nation, fhort of his death. It is to be regretted, that the fituation of things was fuch, that his death could not be voted by the whole nation, or their reprefentatives folemnly affembled for that purpofe. Such a tranfaction would have been an immortal honour to this country, whenever the fuperftitious notion of the *facrednefs of kingly power* fhall be obliterated. A notion which has been extremely ufeful in the infant ftate of focieties; but which,

like

like other fuperftitions, fubfifts long after
it hath ceafed to be of ufe.

The fum of what hath been advanced
upon this head, is a maxim, than which
nothing is more true, that *every government, whatever be the form of it, is originally, and antecedent to its prefent form,
an equal republic*; and, confequently,
that every man, when he comes to be
fenfible of his natural rights, and to feel
his own importance, will confider himfelf as fully equal to any other perfon
whatever. The confideration of riches
and power, however acquired, muft be
entirely fet afide, when we come to thefe
firft principles. The very idea of property, or right of any kind, is founded
upon a regard to the general good of the
fociety, under whofe protection it is enjoyed; and nothing is properly *a man's
own*, but what general rules, which have
for their object the good of the whole,
give to him. To whomfoever the fociety delegates its power, it is delegated
to

to them for the more eafy management of public affairs, and in order to make the more effectual provifion for the happinefs of the whole. Whoever enjoys property, or riches in the ftate, enjoys them for the good of the ftate, as well as for himfelf; and whenever thofe powers, riches, or rights of any kind, are abufed, to the injury of the whole, that awful and ultimate tribunal, in which every citizen hath an equal voice, may demand the refignation of them; and in circumftances, where regular commiffions from this abufed public cannot be had, every man, who has power, and who is actuated with the fentiments of the public, may affume a public character, and bravely redrefs public wrongs. In fuch difmal and critical circumftances, the ftifled voice of an oppreffed country is a loud call upon every man, poffeffed with a fpirit of patriotifm, to exert himfelf; and whenever that voice fhall be at liberty, it will ratify

tify and applaud the action, which it could not formally authorize.

In large ftates, this ultimate feat of power, this tribunal to which lies an appeal from every other, and from which no appeal can even be imagined, is too much hid, and kept out of fight by the prefent complex forms of government, which derive their authority from it. Hence hath arifen a want of clear-nefs and confiftency in the language of the friends of liberty. Hence the pre-pofterous and flavifh maxim, that whatever is enacted by that body of men, in whom the fupreme power of the ftate is vefted, muft, in all cafes, be implicitly obeyed; and that no attempt to repeal an unjuft law can be vindi-cated, beyond a fimple remonftrance addreffed to the legiflators. A cafe, which is very intelligible, but which can never happen, will demonftrate the abfurdity of fuch a maxim.

Sup-

Suppoſe the king of England, and the two houſes of parliament, ſhould make a law, in all the uſual forms, to exempt the members of either houſe from paying taxes to the government, or to appropriate to themſelves the property of their fellow citizens. A law like this would open the eyes of the whole nation, and ſhow them the true principles of government, and the power of governors. The nation would ſee that the moſt regular governments might become tyrannical, and their governors oppreſſive, by ſeparating their intereſt from that of the people whom they governed. Such a law would ſhow them to be but ſervants, and ſervants who had ſhamefully abuſed their truſt. In ſuch a caſe, every man for himſelf would lay his hand upon his ſword, and the authority of the ſupreme power of the ſtate would be annihilated.

So plain are theſe firſt principles of all government, and political liberty, that

that I will take upon me to fay, it is impoffible a man fhould not be convinced
of them, who brings to the fubject a
mind free from the groffeft and meaneft
prejudices. Whatever be the form of
any government, whoever be the fupreme
magiftrates, or whatever be their number; that is, to whomfoever the power
of the fociety is delegated, their authority is, in its own nature, reverfible. No
man can be fuppofed to refign his natural liberty, but on *conditions*. Thefe
conditions, whether they be expreffed or
not, muft be violated, whenever the
plain and obvious ends of government
are not anfwered; and a delegated power,
perverted from the intention for which
it was beftowed, expires of courfe. Magiftrates, therefore, who confult not the
good of the public, and who employ
their power to opprefs the people, are a
public nuifance, and their power is abro-
gated *ipfo facto*.

This, however, can only be the cafe
in extreme oppreffion; when the bleffings

fings of fociety and civil government,
great and important as they are, are
bought too dear; when it is better not
to be governed at all than to be governed in fuch a manner; or, at leaft,
when the hazard of a change of government would be apparently the lefs
evil of the two; and, therefore, thefe
occafions rarely occur in the courfe of
human affairs. It may be afked, what
fhould a people do in cafe of lefs general
oppreffion, and only particular grie-
vances; when the deputies of the people
make laws which evidently favour
themfelves, and bear hard upon the
body of the people they reprefent, and
fuch as they would certainly difapprove,
could they be affembled for that purpofe? I anfwer, that when this appears
to be very clearly the cafe, as it ought
by all means to do (fince, in many cafes,
if the government have not power to
enforce a bad law, it will not have
power to enforce a good one) the firft
ftep which a wife and moderate people
will take is to make a remonftrance to
the

the legiflature; and if that be not practicable, or be not heard; ftill, if the complaints be general, and loud, a wife prince and miniftry will pay regard to them; or they will, at length, be weary of enforcing a penal law which is generally abhorred and difregarded; when they fee the people will run the rifque of the punifhment, if it cannot be evaded, rather than quietly fubmit to the injunction. And a regard to the good of fociety will certainly juftify this conduct of the people.

If an over fcrupulous confcience fhould prevent the people from expreffing their fentiments in this manner, there is no method left, until an opportunity offers of chufing honefter deputies, in which the voice of the loweft claffes can be heard, in order to obtain the appeal of an oppreffive law.

Governors will never be awed by the voice of the people, fo long as it is a
mere

mere voice, without overt-acts. The
confequence of thefe feemingly moderate maxims is, that a door will be left
open to all kinds of oppreffion, without
any refource or redrefs, till the public
wrongs be accumulated to the degree
above mentioned, when all the world
would juftify the utter fubverfion of the
government. Thefe maxims, therefore, admit of no remedy but the laft,
and moft hazardous of all. But is not
even a mob a lefs evil than a rebellion,
and ought the former to be fo feverely
blamed by writers on this fubject, when
it may prevent the latter? Of two evils
of any kind, political as well as others,
it is the dictate of common fenfe to
chufe the lefs. Befides, according to
common notions, avowed by writers
upon morals on lefs general principles,
and by lawyers too, all penal laws give
a man an alternative, either to abftain
from the action prohibited, or to take
the penalty.

PART

PART II.

OF

CIVIL LIBERTY.

SECT. I.

Of the nature of Civil Liberty in general.

IT is a matter of the greateſt importance, that we carefully diſtinguiſh
between the *form*, and the *extent of power*
in a government; for many maxims in
politics depend upon the one, which
are too generally aſcribed to the other.

It is comparatively of ſmall conſequence *who*, or *how many* be our gover-

nors,

nors, or *how long* their office conti-
nues, provided their power be the fame
while they are in office, and the adminiftration be uniform and certain. All
the difference which can arife to ftates
from diverfities, in the number or duration of governors, can only flow from
the motives and opportunities, which
thofe different circumftances may give
their deputies, of extending, or making
a bad ufe of their power. But whether
a people enjoy more or fewer of their
natural rights, under any form of government, is a matter of the laft importance; and upon this depends, what,
I fhould chufe to call, the *civil liberty* of
the ftate, as diftinct from its political
liberty.

If the power of government be very
extenfive, and the fubjects of it have,
confequently, little power over their
own actions, that government is tyrannical, and oppreffive; whether, with refpect to its form, it be a monarchy, an
arifto-

ariftocracy, or even a republic. For the
government of the temporary magiftrates of a democracy, or even the laws
themfelves may be as tyrannical as the
maxims of the moft defpotic monarchy,
and the adminiftration of the government may be as deftructive of private
happinefs. The only confolation that a
democracy fuggefts in thofe circumftances is, that every member of the ftate
has a chance of arriving at a fhare in the
chief magiftracy, and confequently of
playing the tyrant in his turn; and as
there is no government in the world fo
perfectly democratical, as that every
member of the ftate, without exception,
has a right of being admitted into the
adminiftration, great numbers will be
in the fame condition as if they had lived
under the moft abfolute monarchy; and
this is, in fact, almoft univerfally the
cafe with the poor, in all governments.

For

For the fame reafon, if there were no fixed laws, but every thing was decided according to the will of the perfons in power; who is there that would think it of much confequence, whether his life, his liberty, or his property were at the mercy of one, of a few, or of a great number of people, that is, of a mob, liable to the worft of influences. So far, therefore, we may fafely fay, with Mr. Pope, that *thofe governments which are beft adminiftered are beft:*—that is, provided the power of government be moderate, and leave a man the moft valuable of his private rights ; provided the laws be certainly known to every one, and the adminiftration of them be uniform, it is of no confequence how many, or how few perfons are employed in the adminiftration. But it muft be allowed, that there is not the fame chance for the continuance of fuch laws, and of fuch an adminiftration, whether the power be lodged in few, or in more hands.

The

The governments now fubfifting in Europe differ widely in their forms; but it is certain, that the prefent happinefs of the fubjects of them can by no means be eftimated by a regard to the form, but that it depends chiefly upon the power, the extent, and the maxims of government, refpecting perfonal fecurity, private property, &c. and on the certainty and uniformity of the administration.

Civil liberty has been greatly impaired by an abufe of the maxim, that the joint underftanding of all the members of a ftate, properly collected, muft be preferable to that of individuals; and confequently that the more the cafes are, in which mankind are governed by this united reafon of the whole community, fo much the better; whereas, in truth, the greater part of human actions are of fuch a nature, that more inconveniences would follow from their being fixed by

E 3   laws,

laws, than from their being left to every man's arbitrary will.

Political and civil liberty, as before explained, though very different, have, however, a very near and manifeft connection ; and the former is the chief guard of the latter, and on that account, principally, is valuable, and worth contending for. If all the political power of this country were lodged in the hands of one perfon, and the government thereby changed into an abfolute monarchy, the people would find no difference, provided the fame laws, and the fame adminiftration, which now fubfift, were continued. But then, the people, having no political liberty, would have no fecurity for the continuance of the fame laws, and the fame adminiftration. They would have no guard for their civil liberty. The monarch, having it in his option, might not chufe to continue the fame laws, and the fame adminiftration.

miniftration. He might fancy it to be for his own intereft to alter them, and to abridge his fubjects in their private rights ; and, in general, it may be depended upon, that governors will not confult the intereft of the people, except it be their own intereft too, becaufe governors are but men. But while a number of the people have a fhare in the legiflature, fo as to be able to control the fupreme magiftrate, there is a great probability that things will continue in a good ftate. For the more political liberty the people have, the fafer is their civil liberty.

Befides, political and civil liberty have many things in common, which indeed, is the reafon why they have been fo often confounded. A fenfe both of political and civil flavery makes a man think meanly of himfelf. The feeling of his infignificance debafes his mind, checks every great and enterprifing fentiment ; and, in fact, renders him that

poor

poor abject creature, which he fancies himfelf to be. Having always fome unknown evil to fear, though it fhould never come, he has no perfect enjoyment of himfelf, or of any of the bleffings of life; and thus, his fentiments and his enjoyments being of a lower kind, the man finks nearer to the ftate of the brute creation.

On the other hand, a fenfe of political and civil liberty, though there fhould be no great occafion to exert it in the courfe of a man's life, gives him a con-ftant feeling of his own power and im-portance; and is the foundation of his indulging a free, bold, and manly turn of thinking, unreftrained by the moft diftant idea of control. Being free from all fear, he has the moft perfect enjoy-ment of himfelf, and of all the bleffings of life; and his fentiments and enjoy-ments, being raifed, his very *being* is ex-alted, and the man makes nearer ap-proaches to fuperior natures.

The

The hiftory of all antient and modern nations confirms thefe remarks. " In " travelling through Germany," fays Lady M. W. Montague, " it is im- " poffible not to obferve the difference " between the free towns, and thofe " under the government of abfolute " princes, as all the little fovereigns of " Germany are. In the firft there ap- " pears an air of commerce and plenty, " the ftreets are well built, and full of " people, the fhops are loaded with " merchandize, and the commonalty " are clean and chearful. In the other, " you fee a fort of fhabby finery, a " number of people of quality tawdried " out, narrow nafty ftreets, out of repair, " wretchedly thin of inhabitants, and " above half of the common people " afking alms." Lady M. W. Montague's Letters, vol. I. page 16.

" Every houfe in Turkey," the fame excellent writer obferves, " at the death " of its mafter, is at the grand feignor's " difpo-

" difpofal; and therefore no man cares
" to make a great expence, which he is
" not fure his family will be the better
" for. All their defign is to build a
" houfe commodious, and that will laft
" their lives, and they are very indif-
" ferent if it falls down the next year."
Ib. p. 70.

" The fear of the laws," fays the ad-
mirable author of the Effay on crimes
and punifhments, " is falutary, but the
" fear of man is a fruitful and fatal
" fource of crimes. Men enflaved are
" more voluptuous, more debauched,
" and more cruel than thofe who are in
" a ftate of freedom. Thefe ftudy the
" fciences, and the interefts of nations.
" They have great objects before their
" eyes, and imitate them. But thofe
" whofe views are confined to the pre-
" fent moment, endeavour, amidft the
" diftraction of riot and debauchery, to
" forget their fituation. Accuftomed to
" the uncertainty of all events, the con-
                            " fequences

" fequences of their crimes become pro-
" blematical; which gives an additional
" force to the ftrength of their paffions."
Effay on crimes and punifhments, page
166.

The proper extent of civil government, at the fame time that it is a thing
of the greateft confequence, is, neverthelefs, not eafy to be circumfcribed
within narrow limits; becaufe mankind
are not agreed with refpect to one particular circumftance, refpecting the proper object of civil government, which
muft be previoufly fixed. That the
happinefs of the whole community is
the ultimate end of government can
never be doubted, and all claims of individuals inconfiftent with the public
good are abfolutely null and void; but
there is a real difficulty in determining
what general rules, refpecting the extent of the power of government, or
of governors, are moft conducive to the
public good.

Some

Some may think it beſt, that the legiſlature ſhould make exprefs proviſion
for every thing which can even indirectly, remotely, and confequentially, affect
the public good; while others may think
it beſt, that every thing, which is not
properly of a civil nature, ſhould be
entirely overlooked by the civil magiſtrate; that it is for the advantage of
the ſociety, upon the whole, that all
thoſe things be left to take their own
natural courſe, and that the legiſlature
cannot interfere in them, without de-
feating its own great object, the public
good.

We are ſo little capable of arguing
a priori in matters of government, that
it ſhould ſeem, experiments only can
determine how far this power of the legiſlature ought to extend, and it ſhould
likewiſe ſeem, that, till a ſufficient
number of experiments have been made,
it becomes the wiſdom of the civil magiſtracy to take as little upon its hands
as

as poſſible, and never to interfere, without the greateſt caution, in things that do not immediately affect the lives, liberty, or property of the members of the community; that civil magiſtrates ſhould hardly ever be moved to exert themſelves by the mere *tendencies of things,* thoſe tendencies are generally ſo vague, and often ſo imaginary; and that nothing but a manifeſt and urgent neceſſity (of which, however, themſelves are, to be ſure, the only judges) can juſtify them in extending their authority to whatever has no more than a tendency, though the ſtrongeſt poſſible, to diſturb the tranquility and happineſs of the ſtate.

There is, with me, no doubt, but that any people, forming themſelves into a ſociety, may ſubject themſelves to whatever reſtrictions they pleaſe; and conſequently, that the ſupreme civil magiſtrates, on whom the whole power of the ſociety is devolved, may make
what

what laws they pleafe; but the queftion
is, what reftrictions and laws are wife,
and calculated to promote the public
good; for fuch only are juft, right, and,
properly fpeaking, lawful.

SECT. II.

*In what manner an authoritative code
of education would affect liberty and
focial happinefs.*

HAVING confidered the nature
of civil liberty in general, I
fhall treat of two capital branches of
which it confifts, in two diftinct fecti-
ons. Thefe are the rights of education,
and religion. On thefe two articles
much of the happinefs of human life is
acknowledged to depend; but they appear to me to be of fuch a nature, that
the advantage we derive from them will
be more effectually fecured, when they
are

are conducted by individuals, than by the state; and if this can be demonstrated, nothing more is necessary, to prove that the civil magistrate has no business to interfere with them.

This I cannot help thinking to be the shortest, and the best issue upon which we can put every thing in which the civil magistrate pretends to a right of interference. If it be probable that the business, whatever it be, will be conducted better, that is, more to the advantage of society, in his hands, than in those of individuals, the right will be allowed. In those circumstances, it is evident, that no friend to society can deny his claim. But if the nature of the thing be such that the attention of individuals, with respect to it, can be applied to more advantage than that of the magistrate; the claim of the former must be admitted, in preference to that of the latter.

No

No doubt, there are examples of both kinds The avenging of injuries, or redreffing of private wrongs, is certainly better trufted in the hands of the magiftrate than in thofe of private perfons; but with what advantage could a magiftrate interfere in a thoufand particulars relating to private families, and private friendfhips. Now I think it is clear, that education muft be ranked in the latter clafs, or among thofe things in which the civil magiftrate has no right to interfere; becaufe he cannot do it to any good purpofe. But fince Dr. Brown has lately maintained the contrary in a treatife, intitled, *Thoughts on civil liberty, licentioufnefs, and faction,* and in an *Appendix relative to a propofed code of education,* fubjoined to a *Sermon on the female character and education.* I fhall in this fection, reply to what he has advanced on this fubject, and offer what has occurred to me with relation to it.

Left

Left it fhould be apprehended, that I miftake the views of this writer, I fhall fubjoin a few extracts from the work, which contain the fubftance of what he has advanced on the fubject of education. He afferts, " That, the firft and beft fe-
" curity of civil liberty confifts, in im-
" preffing the infant mind with fuch ha-
" bits of thought and action, as may cor-
" refpond with, and promote the ap-
" pointments of public law." In his appendix, he fays, that, " by a CODE OF
" EDUCATION, he means a fyftem of
" principles, religious, moral, and poli-
" tical, whofe tendency may be the pre-
" fervation of the bleffings of fociety, as
" they are enjoyed in a free ftate, to be
" inftilled effectually into the infant and
" growing minds of the community, for
" this great end of public happinefs"

In what manner the fecurity of civil liberty is to be effected by means of this code of education, may be feen in the following defcription he gives of the inftitutions

tutions of Sparta. " No father had a
" right to educate his children accord-
" ing to the caprice of his own fancy.
" They were delivered to public officers,
" who initiated them early in the man-
" ners, the maxims, the exercifes, the
" toils ; in a word, in all the mental and
" bodily acquirements and habits which
" correfponded with the genius of the
" ftate. Family connections had no
" place. The firft and leading object
" of their affection was the general wel-
" fare. This tuition was carefully con-
" tinued till they were enrolled in the
" lift of men."

With refpect to the Athenian government, he fays, page 62, " The firft and
" ruling defect in the inftitution of this
" republic feems to have been the total
" want of an eftablifhed education, fui-
" table to the genius of the ftate. There
" appears not to have been any public,
" regular, or prefcribed appointment of
" this kind, beyond what cuftom had
" accidentally introduced."

He

He fays, page 70, " There were three
" fatal circumftances admitted into the
" very effence of the Roman republic,
" which contained the feeds of certain
" ruin; the firft of which was, the neg-
" lect of inftituting public laws, by
" which the education of their children
" might have been afcertained."

He complains, page 83, " that the
" Britifh fyftem of policy and religion
" is not upheld in its native power like
" that of Sparta, by correfpondent and
" effectual rules of education; that it is
" in the power of every private man to
" educate his child, not only without a
" reverence for thefe, but in abfolute
" contempt of them; that, at the re-
" volution, page 90, the education of
" youth was ftill left in an imperfect
" ftate; this great revolution having
" confined itfelf to the reform of public
" inftitutions, without afcending to the
" great fountain of political fecurity,
" the private and effectual formation of

F 2   " the

" the infant mind ; and, page 107, that
" education was afterwards left ftill
" more and more imperfect."

Laftly, he afferts, page 156, " that
" the chief and effential remedy of licen-
" tioufnefs and faction, the fundamental
" means of the lafting and fecure eftab-
" lifhment of civil liberty, can only be in
" a general and prefcribed improvement
" of the laws of education, to which all
" the members of the community fhould
" legally fubmit ; and that for want of
" a prefcribed code of education, the
" manners and principles, on which
" alone the ftate can reft, are in-
" effectually inftilled, are vague, fluc-
" tuating and felf contradictory. No-
" thing," he fays, " is more evident, than
" that fome reform in this great point is
" neceffary for the fecurity of public free-
" dom; and that though it is an incurable
" defect of our political ftate, that it has
" not a correfpondent and adequate code
" of education inwrought into its firft
                                    " effence;

" effence ; we may yet hope, that, in a
" fecondary and inferior degree, fome-
" thing of this kind may ftill be inlaid ;
" that, though it cannot have that perfect
" efficacy, as if it had been originally of
" the piece, yet, if well conducted, it
" may ftrengthen the weak parts, and al-
" leviate defects, if not completely re-
" move them."

In conducting my examination of thefe
fentiments, I fhall make no remarks upon
any particular paffages in the book, but
confider only the author's general fcheme,
and the proper and profeffed object of it.
And as the doctor has propofed no particular plan of public education, I fhall
be as general as he has been, and only
fhew the inconvenience of eftablifhing,
by law, any plan of education whatever.

This writer pleads for a plan of education eftablifhed by the legiflature, as the
only effectual method of preventing faction in the ftate, and fecuring the perpetui-

ty

ty of our excellent conftitution, ecclefiaftical and civil. I agree with him, in ac-
knowledging the importance of education, as influencing the manners and the
conduct of men. I alfo acknowledge,
that an uniform plan of education, agreeable to the principles of any particular
form of government, civil or ecclefiaftical, would tend to eftablifh and perpetuate that form of government, and prevent
civil diffentions and factions in the ftate.
But I fhould object to the interference of
the legiflature in this bufinefs of education,
as prejudicial to the proper defign of education, and alfo to the great ends of civil
focieties with refpect to their prefent
utility. I fhall moreover fhow, that it
would be abfolutely inconfiftent with the
true principles of the Englifh government, and could not be carried into execution, to any purpofe, without the ruin
of our prefent conftitution. I beg the
candour of the public, while I endeavour to explain, in as few words as poffible, in what manner, I apprehend, this
inter-

interference of the civil magiftrate would operate to obftruct thefe great ends. I fhall confider thefe articles feparately.

I obferved in the firft place, that I ap- prehended a legal code of education might interfere with the proper defign of educa- tion. I do not mean what this writer feems to confider as the only object of education, the tranquility of the ftate, but the forming of wife and virtuous men; which is certainly an object of the great- eft importance in every ftate. If the conftitution of a ftate be a good one, fuch men will be the greateft bulwarks of it; if it be a bad one, they will be the moft able and ready to contribute to its reformation; in either of which cafes they will render it the greateft fervice.

Education is as much an art (founded, as all arts are, upon fcience) as hufban- dry, as architecture, or as fhip-building. In all thefe cafes we have a practical pro- blem propofed to us, which muft be per-
F 4   formed

formed by the help of *data* with which experience and obfervation furnifh us. The end of fhip-building is to make the beft fhips, of architecture the beft houfes, and of education, the beft men. Now, of all arts, thofe ftand the faireft chance of being brought to perfection, in which there is opportunity of making the moft experiments and trials, and in which there are the greateft number and variety of perfons employed in making them. Hiftory and experience fhow, that, *cæteris paribus*, thofe arts have always, in fact, been brought the fooneft, or the neareft to perfection, which have been placed in thofe favourable circumftances. The reafon is, that the operations of the human mind are flow ; a number of falfe hypothefes and conclufions always precede the right one ; and in every art, manual or liberal, a number of awkward attempts are made, before we are able to execute any thing which will bear to be fhown as a mafter-piece in the art ; fo that to eftablifh the methods and pro-

ceffes

ceffes of any art, before it have arrived
to a ftate of perfection (of which no man
can be a judge) is to fix it in its infancy,
to perpetuate every thing that is inconve-
nient and awkward in it, and to cut off its
future growth and improvement. And
to eftablifh the methods and proceffes of
any art when it has arrived to perfection
is fuperfluous. It will then recommend and eftablifh itfelf.

Now I appeal to any perfon whether
any plan of education, which has yet been
put in execution in this kingdom, be fo
perfect as that the eftablifhing of it by
authority would not obftruct the great
ends of education; or even whether the
united genius of man could, at prefent,
form fo perfect a plan. Every man who
is experienced in the bufinefs of education
well knows, that the art is in its infancy; but advancing, it is hoped, apace to
a ftate of manhood. In this condition,
it requires the aid of every circumftance
favourable to its natural growth, and
dreads

dreads nothing fo much as being confined
and cramped by the unfeafonable hand of
power. To put it (in its prefent imperfect ftate) into the hands of the civil magiftrate, in order to fix the mode of it,
would be like fixing the drefs of a child,
and forbidding its cloaths ever to be made
wider or larger.

Manufacturers and artifts of feveral
kinds already complain of the obftruc-
tion which is given to their arts, by the
injudicious acts of former parliaments;
and it is the object of our wifeft ftatefmen
to get thefe obftructions removed, by the
repeal of thofe acts. I wifh it could not
be faid, that the bufinefs of education is
already under too many legal reftraints.
Let thefe be removed, and a few more
fair experiments made of the different
methods of conducting it, before the legiflature think proper to interfere any
more with it, and by that time, it is
hoped, they will fee no reafon to interfere at all. The bufinefs would be conducted

ducted to much better purpofe, even in favour of their own views, if thofe views were juft and honourable, than it would be under any arbitrary regulations whatever.

To fhew this fcheme of an eftablifhed method of education in a clearer point of light, let us imagine that what is now propofed had been carried into execution fome centuries before this time. For no reafon can be affigned for fixing any mode of education at prefent, which might not have been made ufe of, with the fame appearance of reafon, for fixing another approved method a thoufand years ago. Suppofe Alfred, when he founded the univerfity of Oxford, had made it impoffible, that the method of inftruction ufed in his time fhould ever have been altered. Excellent as that method might have been, for the time in which it was inftituted, it would now have been the worft method that is practifed in the world. Suppofe the number of the arts and fci-

ences

ences, with the manner of teaching them, had been fixed in this kingdom, before the revival of letters and of the arts, it is plain they could never have arrived at their prefent advanced ftate among us. We fhould not have had the honour to lead the way in the moft noble difcoveries, in the mathematics, philofophy, aftronomy, and, I may add, divinity too. And for the fame reafon, were fuch an eftablifhment to take place in the prefent age, it would prevent all great improvements in futurity.

I may add, in this place, that, if we argue from the analogy of education to other arts which are moft fimilar to it, we can never expect to fee human nature, about which it is employed, brought to perfection, but in confequence of indulging unbounded liberty, and even caprice in conducting it. The power of nature in producing plants cannot be fhown to advantage, but in all poffible circumftances of culture. The richeft colours, the

moft

moft fragrant fcents and the moft ex-
quifite flavours, which our prefent gar-
dens and orchards exhibit, would never have been known, if florifts and gar-
deners had been confined in the proceffes
of cultivation; nay if they had not been
allowed the utmoft licentioufnefs of fancy
in the exercife of their arts. Many of
the fineft productions of modern garden-
ing have been the refult of cafual experiment, perhaps of undefigned deviation
from eftablifhed rules. Obfervations of
a fimilar nature may be made on the methods of breeding cattle, and training
animals of all kinds. And why fhould
the rational part of the creation be deprived of that opportunity of diverfifying
and improving itfelf, which the vegetable
and animal world enjoy?

From new, and feemingly irregular methods of education, perhaps fomething
extraordinary and uncommonly great may
fpring. At leaft there would be a fair
chance for fuch productions; and if fomething odd and excentric fhould, now and
then,

then, arife from this unbounded liberty of education, the various bufinefs of human life may afford proper fpheres for fuch excentric geniufes.

Education, taken in its moft extenfive fenfe, is properly that which makes the man. One method of education, therefore, would only produce one kind of men; but the great excellence of human nature confifts in the variety of which it is capable. Inftead then of endeavouring, by uniform and fixed fyftems of education, to keep mankind always the fame, let us give free fcope to every thing which may bid fair for introducing more variety among us. The various character of the Athenians was certainly preferable to the uniform character of the Spartans, or to any uniform national character whatever.

Is it not univerfally confidered as an advantage to England, that it contains fo great a variety of original characters? And

And is it not, on this account, preferred to France, Spain, or Italy?

Uniformity is the characteristic of the brute creation. Among them every species of birds build their nests with the same materials, and in the same form; the genius and disposition of one individual is that of all; and it is only the education which men give them that raises any of them much above others. But it is the glory of human nature, that the operations of reason, though variable, and by no means infallible, are capable of infinite improvement. We come into the world worse provided than any of the brutes, and for a year or two of our lives, many of them go far beyond us in intellectual accomplishments. But when their faculties are at a full stand, and their enjoyments incapable of variety, or increase, our intellectual powers are growing apace; we are perpetually deriving happiness from new sources, and even before

we

we leave this world are capable of taſt-
ing the felicity of angels.

Have we, then, ſo little ſenſe of the
proper excellence of our natures, and of
the views of divine providence in our formation, as to catch at a poor advantage a-
dapted to the lower nature of brutes. Rather, let us hold on in the courſe in
which the divine being himſelf has put
us, by giving reaſon its full play, and
throwing off the fetters which ſhort-
ſighted and ill-judging men have hung
upon it. Though, in this courſe, we be
liable to more extravagancies than brutes,
governed by blind but unerring inſtinct,
or than men whom miſtaken ſyſtems of
policy have made as uniform in their ſentiments and conduct as the brutes, we
ſhall be in the way to attain a degree of
perfection and happineſs of which they
can have no idea.

However, as men are firſt animals before they can be properly termed rational
crea-

creatures, and the analogies of individuals extend to focieties, a principle fomething refembling the inftinct of animals
may, perhaps, fuit mankind in their infant ftate; but then, as we advance in
the arts of life, let us, as far as we are
able, affert the native freedom of 'our
fouls, and, after having been fervilely governed like brutes, afpire to the noble
privilege of governing ourfelves like
men.

If it may have been neceffary to eftablifh fomething by law concerning education, that neceffity grows lefs every
day, and encourages us to relax the bonds
of authority, rather than bind them
fafter.

Secondly, this fcheme of an eftablifhed mode of education would be prejudicial to the great ends of civil fociety.
The great object of civil fociety is the
happinefs of the members of it, in the
perfect and undifturbed enjoyment of

G   the

the more important of our natural rights, for the fake of which, we voluntarily give up others of lefs confequence to us. But whatever be the bleffings of civil fociety, they may be bought too dear. It is certainly poffible to facrifice too much, at leaft more than is neceffary to be facrificed for them, in order to produce the greateft fum of happinefs in the community. Elfe why do we complain of tyrannical and oppreffive governments? Is it not the meaning of all complaints of this kind, that, in fuch governments, the fubjects are deprived of their moft important natural rights, without an equivalent recompence; that all the valuable ends of civil government might be effectually fecured, and the members of particular ftates be much happier upon the whole, if they did not lie under thofe reftrictions.

Now, of all the fources of happinefs and enjoyment in human life, the domeftic relations are the moft conftant

and

and copious. With our wives and children we neceſſarily paſs the greateſt part
of our lives. The connections of friend-
ſhip are ſlight in compariſon of this inti-
mate domeſtic union. Views of intereſt
or ambition may divide the neareſt
friends, but our wives and children are,
in general, inſeparably connected with
us and attached to us. With them all
our joys are doubled, and in their affection and aſſiduity we find conſolation under all the troubles and diſquietudes of
life. For the enjoyments which reſult
from this moſt delightful intercourſe, all
mankind, in all ages, have been ready to
ſacrifice every thing; and for the inter-
ruption of this intercourſe no compenſa-
tion whatever can be made by man.
What then can be more juſtly alarming
to a man who has a true taſte for happineſs, than, either that the choice of his
wife, or the education of his children
ſhould be under the direction of perſons
who have no particular knowledge of him,
or particular affection for him, and whoſe

G 2   views

views and maxims he might utterly dif-
like? What profpect of happinefs could
a man have with fuch a wife, or fuch
children?

It is poffible, indeed, that the prefer-
vation of fome civil focieties, fuch as that
of Sparta, may require this facrifice ; but
thofe civil focieties muft be wretchedly
conftituted to ftand in need of it, and had
better be utterly diffolved. Were I a
member of fuch a ftate, thankful fhould I
be to its governors, if they would permit
me peaceably to retire to any other
country, where fo great a facrifice was
not required. Indeed, it is hardly poffible that a ftate fhould require facrifice,
which I fhould think of fo much importance. And, I doubt not; fo many others
would be of the fame mind, that there
would foon be very little reafon to complain of the too great increafe of commerce in fuch a country. This, however, would render very neceffary another part of our author's fcheme ; viz.
putting

putting a reftraint upon travelling abroad, left too many perfons fhould be willing to leave fuch a country, and have no inclination to return.

If there be any natural rights which ought not to be facrificed to the ends of civil fociety, and no politicians or moral-ifts deny but that there are fome (the obligations of religion, for inftance, being certainly of a fuperior nature) it is even more natural to look for thefe rights among thofe which refpect a man's chil-dren, than among thofe which refpect himfelf; becaufe nature has generally made them dearer to him than him-felf.

If any truft can be faid to be of God, and fuch as ought not to be relinquifhed at the command of man, it is that which we have of the education of our chil-dren, which the divine being feems to have put under our immediate care; that we may inftruct them in fuch principles,

G 3   form

form them to fuch manners, and give them fuch habits of thinking and acting, as we fhall judge to be of the greateft importance to their prefent and future well being.

I believe there is no father in the world (who, to a fenfe of religion, joins a ftrong fenfe of parental affection) who would think his own liberty above half indulged to him, when abridged in fo tender a point, as that of providing, to his own fatisfaction, for the good conduct and happinefs of his offspring. Nature feems to have eftablifhed fuch a ftrong connexion between a parent and his children, at leaft during the firft period of their lives, that to drag them from the afylum of their natural guardians, to force them to public places of education, and to inftil into them religious fentiments contrary to the judgment and choice of their parents, would be as cruel, as obliging a man to make the greateft
perfonal

perſonal ſacrifice, even that of his conſcience, to the civil magiſtrate.

What part of the perſecution which
the proteſtants in France underwent
did they complain of more feelingly, and
with more juſtice, than that of their children being forced from them, and carried to be educated in public monaſteries?
God forbid that the parental affections
of free born Britons ſhould ever be put to
ſo ſevere a trial! or to that which the
poor Jews in Portugal ſuffered; many of
whom cut the throats of their children,
or threw them into wells, and down pre-
cipices, rather than ſuffer them to be
dragged away to be educated under the
direction of a popiſh inquiſition; thinking the lives of their children a leſs ſacrifice than that of their principles.

It was a meaſure ſimilar to that which
Dr. Brown recommended, at which the
whole chriſtian world took the greateſt
alarm that was ever given to it, in the

reign

reign of that great man, but inveterate enemy of chriftianity, the emperor Julian; who would have fhut up the fchools of chriftians, and have forbidden them to teach rhetoric and philofophy. Similar to this fcheme, in its nature and tendency, was the moft odious meafure of the moft odious miniftry that ever fat at the helm of the Britifh government, and which was providentially defeated the very day that it was to have been carried into execution; I mean the schism bill, patronized by the Tory minifters in the latter end of the reign of queen Ann. Should thefe meafures be refumed, and purfued, Farewel, a long farewel to England's greatnefs! Nor would this be faid in a hafty fit of unreafonable defpair. For, befides that fuch a meafure as this could not but have many extenfive confequences; it is not to be doubted, but that whoever they be who do thus much, they both can and will do more. Such a fcheme as this will never be pufhed for its own fake only.

In

In examining the prefent operation
and utility of any fcheme of policy, we
ought to take into confideration the eafe
or the difficulty of carrying it into execution. For if the difturbance, which
would be occafioned by bringing it into
execution, would be fo great an inconvenience, as to overbalance the good to
be effected by it, it were better never to
attempt it. Now, though the doctor
hath laid down no particular fcheme of
public and eftablifhed education, and
therefore we cannot judge of the particular difficulties which would attend the
eftablifhing of it; yet, if it be fuch as
would anfwer the end propofed by him,
this difficulty would appear to me abfolutely infuperable, in fuch a country as
England.

Whatever be the *religious, moral, and
political principles,* which are thought
conducive to the good of the fociety, if
they muft be *effectually inftilled into the
infant and growing minds of the community,*

it

it can never be done without taking the children very early from their parents, and cutting off all communication with them, till they be arrived to maturity and their judgments be abſolutely fixed. And if this author judged, that the reaſon why a ſcheme of this nature did not take place in Athens, was the difficulty of eſtabliſhing it, after the people were tole rably civilized; he muſt certainly judge it to be infinitely more difficult, among a people ſo much farther advanced in the arts of life than the Athenians.

He well obſerves, page 53, that, " to " give children a public education where " no education had taken place, was natu- " ral and practicable;" but he ſeems to be aware, that an attempt to carry any ſuch plan into execution, in the moſt flouriſh- ing period of a free and civilized ſtate, would be highly unnatural, without the leaſt probable hope of ſucceſs, and dan- gerous to ſuch as took it in hand. For he ſays, page 52, that, " to effect a
" change

" change of government only is a work
" fufficient for the abilities of the greateft
" legiflator; but to overturn all the pre-
" eftablifhed habits of the head and
" heart, to deftroy or reverfe all the
" fixed affociations, maxims, manners,
" and principles, were a labour which
" might well be ranked among the
" moft extravagant legends of fabulous
" Greece."

What might be expected from the bufinefs of education being lodged by the
ftate in the hands of any one fet of men,
may be imagined from the alarm which
the Newtonian fyftem gave to all phi-
lofophers at the time of its firft publication, and from what paffed at Oxford
with refpect to Locke's *Effay on the human underftanding*, which hath done fo
much honour to the Englifh nation in
the eyes of all the learned World. We
are told by the authors of *Biographia
Britannica*, in the life of Mr. Locke,
that " there was a meeting of the heads
" of

" of houfes at Oxford, where it was pro-
" pofed to cenfure, and difcourage the
" reading of this Effay; and that, after
" various debates, it was concluded, that,
" without any public cenfure, each head
" of a houfe fhould endeavour to prevent
" its being read in his own college."
This paffed but a little before Mr.
Locke's death, and about fourteen years
after the firft publication of the Effay.

Hitherto I have argued againft eftablifhed modes of education upon general
principles, fhewing how unfavourable
they are to the great ends of civil fociety, with only occafional references to
the Englifh conftitution; and in thefe
arguments I have, likewife, fuppofed
thefe methods of education, whatever
they be, actually eftablifhed, and to have
operated to their full extent. I fhall
now add, that, before thefe methods can
be eftablifhed, and produce their full
effect, they muft occafion a very confiderable alteration in the Englifh conftitution,

tution, and almoft inevitably deftroy the freedom of it; fo that the thing which would, in fact, be perpetuated, would not be the prefent conftitution of England, but fomething very different from it, and more defpotic. An alteration of fo great importance, which tends to defeat one of the principal objects of this government, cannot but give juft caufe of alarm to every friend of the prefent happy conftitution and liberties of this country. In fupport of this affertion, I defire no other argument than that with which Dr. Brown himfelf furnifhes me, from the influence he allows to education, operating, likewife, in the very manner which he defcribes, and to the very end for which he advifes the eftablifhing of its mode.

Education is confidered by the doctor only in a political view, as ufeful to inftil into the minds of youth particular maxims of policy, and to give them an attachment to particular forms of it; or

as

as tending to fuperinduce fuch habits of
mind, and to give fuch a general turn of
thinking, as would correfpond with the
genius of a particular ftate. This education he would have to be univerfal and
uniform; and indeed, if it were not fo,
it could not poffibly anfwer the end propofed. It muft, therefore, be conducted
by one fet of men. But it is impoffible
to find any fet of men, who fhall have
an equal regard to all the parts of our
conftitution; and whatever part is neg-
lected in fuch a fyftem of education it
can not fail to be a fufferer.

The Englifh government is a mixture
of regal, ariftocratical, and democratical
power; and if the public education
fhould be more favourable to any one of
thefe than to another, or more than its
prefent importance in the conftitution
requires, the balance of the whole would
neceffarily be loft. Too much weight
would be thrown into fome of the fcales,
and the conftitution be overturned. If
the

the commons, reprefenting the body of
the people, had the choice of thefe public inftructors, which is almoft impoffible, we fhould fee a republic rife out of
the ruins of our prefent government; if
the lords, which is highly improbable,
we fhould, in the end, have an ariftocracy; and if the court had this nomination, which it may be taken for granted would be the cafe (as all the execu-
tive power of the ftate is already lodged
in the hands of the fovereign) it could
not but occafion a very dangerous acceffion of power to the crown, and we
might juftly expect a fyftem of education,
principles, and manners favourable to
defpotifm. Every man would be educated with principles, which would lead
him to concur with the views of the
court. All that oppofition from the
country, which is fo falutary in this nation, and fo effential to the liberties of
England, would be at an end. And
when once the fpirit of defpotifm was
thus eftablifhed, and had triumphed over
all

all oppofition, we might foon expect to fee the forms of it eftablifhed too, and thereby the very doors fhut againft old Englifh liberty, and effectually guarded againft the poffibility of its return, except by violence; which would then be the only method of its re-entrance.

It is evident to common underftanding, that the true fpirit and maxims of a mixed government can no otherwife be continued, than by every man's educating his children in his own way; and that if any one part provided for the education of the whole, that part would foon gain the afcendency in the whole; and, if it were capable of it, would become the whole. Were a ftate, for inftance, to confift of papifts and proteftants, and the papifts had the fole power of education, proteftantifm would expire with that generation: whereas, if the papifts and proteftants educated each their own children, the fame proportion would continue to fubfift between them, and
the

the balance of power would remain the fame. For the fame reafon the only method of preferving the balance, which at prefent fubfifts among the feveral political and religious parties in Great Britain, is for each party to provide for the education of their own children.

In this way, there will be a fair profpect of things continuing nearly upon their prefent footing, for a confiderable time; but fubject to thofe gradual alterations which, it may be hoped, will prove favourable to the beft interefts of the fociety upon the whole. Whereas, were the direction of the whole bufinefs of education thrown into the hands of the court, it would be fuch an acceffion of power to the regal part of our conftitution, as could not fail to alarm all the friends of civil liberty ; as all the friends of religious liberty would be juftly alarmed, if it fhould devolve upon the eftablifhed clergy. And it were the greateft injuftice to the good fenfe of free born Britons, to fuppofe the noble fpirit

H   of

of religious liberty, and a zeal for the rights of free inquiry confined within the narrow circle of proteſtant diſſenters.

I doubt not, the wiſeſt and the moſt worthy of the Engliſh prelates would rather ſee the privileges of the diſſenters enlarged than abridged, in any important article; for, allowing their diſſent to be ever ſo unreaſonable, there is no man who ·has the leaſt knowledge of hiſtory or of human nature, but muſt be ſenſible, that the very diſtinguiſhed reputation which the body of the Engliſh clergy enjoy at preſent is, not a little, owing to the exiſtence and reſpectable figure of the proteſtant diſſenters. Several of the moſt diſcerning of the Engliſh biſhops have given their teſtimony, directly or indirectly, to this truth; particularly, if I remember right, biſhop Gibſon, in his charges to the clergy of his dioceſs. The preſent ſtate of the diſſenting intereſt can give no alarm to the eſtabliſhed clergy with reſpect to their temporalities; and, certainly,

certainly, the interefts of religious knowledge, which all wife and good men of
every denomination have moft at heart,
cannot fail to be promoted by that fpirit
of emulation, which will always fubfift
betwixt fcholars and writers in two oppofite perfuafions.

There is no power on earth, but has
grown exorbitant when it has met with
no control. What was the character of
the Romifh clergy before the reformation? how fhamefully ignorant, imperi-
ous, lazy, and debauched were the bulk
of them! whereas very great numbers
of them are now fenfible, moderate, and
virtuous; and little, in comparifon, of
the old leaven remains, except in Spain
and Portugal, where the clergy have no
intercourfe with proteftants, which might
call forth an exertion of their faculties,
and check the extravagance of their ap-
petites and paffions. To fay that the
Englifh clergy, in future time, would
not run into the vices, and fink into the

con-

contempt, into which the Romifh clergy were funk before the reformation, when they were in the fame circumftances, would be to fay they were not men.

It is Puffendorf, I think, who accounts for the great fuperiority of the Englifh clergy over the Swedifh upon this principle. In Sweden, though it be a proteftant country, no diffenters are allowed ; and their clergy have never produced anything, in ethics or divinity, which deferves notice. Whoever made the obfervation, there is no doubt of the fact.

A few narrow minded, and fhort-fighted bigots, among the inferior clergy, may wifh the extinction of the diffenting intereft, and might be ready to gratify their hatred and blind zeal, by perfecuting thofe of their brethren whofe confciences are, unhappily, a little more tender than their own; but, certainly, there would not be wanting, in this age, men enow of more humanity, of jufter

fenti-

fentiments, and of more enlarged views, among the higher ranks in the church, who would, with indignation, fnatch the torch from their mifguided hands. Their low talents were better confined to a narrower fphere, in which the fire of their little fouls might very harmlefsly vent itfelf in occafional declamatory invectives; which would only ferve to fhew the malignity of their own tempers, or the meannefs and impotence of bigotry, and make all men of fenfe more in love with the true principles of chriftian moderation. The indelible infamy which would, to the lateft pofterity, purfue the man, who fhould form, countenance, or even connive at, perfecuting meafures, in this age of moderation and good fenfe, will effectually deter men of underftanding, and of a juft knowledge of the world from thefe meafures; and it is hoped, that men of zeal without knowledge will want abilities and influence to carry fuch fchemes into execution.

H 3 No

No nation ever was, or can be truly great, powerful, and happy by purfuing oppreffive and perfecuting meafures. And a fovereign, who has a true fenfe of his prefent and future glory, muft fee it can only arife from his being the head of a great, powerful, and happy nation, made, or continued fo, by himfelf. His beft friends are thofe who would raife his greatnefs, by augmenting the great-nefs of the people over whom he pre-fides. He himfelf muft fee the ab-furdity of every fcheme which propofes to raife his character at the expence of that of his country; as if it were poffible to deprefs the people to the condition of flaves, without finking the fovereign into a mafter of fuch flaves. Poor pre-eminence! fuch maxims may have in-fluence with Afiatic monarchs, but can never impofe on a fovereign of Great-Britain, educated in Britifh principles, and with a juft regard to the privileges of his fubjects, with which his own true dignity is infeparably connected.

The

The nation will execrate, and the dif-
cerning prince will fee through, and de-
teſt the meanneſs of that adulation,which,
however difguifed, would tend to enſlave
the kingdom, and debaſe the king. The
meaneſt tool of the meaneſt party may
exclaim againſt licentioufneſs and faction;
men of genius, learning, and integrity
may, through the force of prejudice, be
induced to join in the cry; and courtiers
may think to recommend themſelves to
a ſovereign by any meaſures which tend
to quiet the clamours of the people ; but
the true enemy of ſedition, and he who
moſt effectually pays his court to a wife
and good prince, is the man, who, without any views of preferment, propoſes,
with a manly freedom, whatever he
thinks conducive to the greatneſs and
glory of his country. This conduct
cannot fail, both to give ſatisfaction to
his fellow citizens, and enſure him the
eſteem of his prince : becauſe ſuch meaſures will proportionably raiſe the luſtre
of all ranks of men in the ſtate, will

make

make a wife prince the idol of a grateful nation, and endear his memory to the lateft pofterity.

Confidering the whole of what hath been advanced in this fection, I think it fufficiently appears, that education is a branch of civil liberty, which ought by no means to be furrendered into the hands of the civil magiftrate, and that the beft interefts of fociety require, that the right of conducting it fhould be inviolably preferved to individuals.

S E C T. III.

Of Religious Liberty and Toleration.

THE moft important queftion concerning the extent of civil government is, whether the civil magiftrate ought to extend his authority to matters of *religion* ; and the only method of

deciding

deciding this important queftion, as it appears to me, is to have recourfe at once to firft principles, and the ultimate rule concerning every thing that refpects a fociety; viz. whether fuch interference of the civil magiftrate appear, from reafon, or from fact, to be for the public good. And as all arguments *a priori* in matters of policy are apt to be fallacious, fact and experience feem to be our only fafe guide. Now thefe, as far as our knowledge of hiftory extends, declare clearly for no interference in this cafe at all, or at leaft for as little as is poffible. Thofe focieties have ever enjoyed the moft happinefs, and have been, *ceteris paribus,* in the moft flourifhing ftate, where the civil magiftrates have meddled the leaft with religion, and where they have the moft clofely confined their attention to what immediately affects the civil interefts of their fellow citizens.

Civil

Civil and religious matters (taking the words in their ufual acceptation) feem to be fo diftinct, that it can only be in very uncommon emergencies, where, for inftance, religious quarrels among the members of the ftate rife very high, that the civil magiftrate can have any call, or pretence, for interfering with religion. We know that infinite mifchiefs have arifen from this interference; and we have yet feen no inconvenience to have arifen from the want, or the relaxation of it.

The fine country of Flanders, the moft flourifhing and opulent then in Europe, was abfolutely ruined, paft recovery, by the mad attempt of Philip the fecond, to introduce the popifh inquifition into that country. France was greatly hurt by the revocation of the edict of Nantz; whereas England was a great gainer on both occafions, by granting an afylum for thofe perfecuted induftrious people; who repaid us for our kindnefs, by the
intro-

introduction of many ufeful arts and ma-
nufactures, which were the foundation
of our prefent commerce, riches, and
power.

Penfylvania flourifhed much more
than New England, or than any other of
the Englifh fettlements in North America, evidently in confequence of giving
more liberty in matters of religion, at its
firft eftablifhment. Holland has found
its advantage in the indulgence fhe gives
to a great variety of religious perfuafions.
England has alfo been much more flourifhing and happy, fince the eftablifhment, as it may properly enough be ftiled,
of the diffenting method of worfhip, by
what is commonly called the *act of tole-*
ration. And all the fenfible part of Europe concur in thinking, both that the
Polifh diffidents have a right to all the
privileges of other Polifh citizens; and
that it is much happier for that country
that their claims are admitted : and
none but interefted bigots oppofed their
demands.

If

If we look a little farther off from home, let it be faid, what inconvenience did Jenghis khan, Tamerlane, and other eaftern conquerors ever find from leaving religion to its natural courfe in the countries they fubdued, and from having chriftians, mahometans, and a variety of pagans under the fame form of civil government? Are not both chriftianity and mohammedanifm, in fact, eftablifhed (the former at leaft fully tolerated) in Turkey; and what inconvenience, worth mentioning, has ever arifen from it?

Pity it is then, that more and fairer experiments are not made; when, judging from what is paft, the confequences of *unbounded liberty, in matters of religion,* promife to be fo very favourable to the beft interefts of mankind.

I am aware, that the connexion between civil and religious affairs, will be urged for the neceffity of fome interference of the legiflature with religion; and

and I do not deny the connection. But as this connection has always been found to be the greateſt in barbarous nations, and imperfect governments, to which it lends an uſeful aid; it may be preſumed, that the connection is gradually growing leſs neceſſary; and that, in the preſent advanced ſtate of human ſociety, there is very little occaſion for it. For my own part, I have no apprehenſion, but that, at this day, the laws might be obeyed very well without any eccleſiaſtical ſanctions, enforced by the civil magiſtrate.

Not that I think religion will ever be a matter of indifference in civil ſociety: that is impoſſible, if the word be underſtood in its greateſt latitude, and by religion we mean that principle whereby men are influenced by the dread of evil, or the hope of reward from any unknown and inviſible cauſes, whether the good or evil be expected to take
place

place in this world or another, compre-
hending enthufiafm, fuperftition, and
every fpecies of falfe religion, as well as
the true. Nor is fuch an event at all defirable; nay, the more juft motives men
have to the fame good actions, the better; but religious motives may ftill operate in favour of the civil laws, without
fuch a connection as has been formed
between them in ecclefiaftical eftablifhments; and, I think, this end would be
anfwered even better without that connection.

In all the modes of religion, which
fubfift among mankind, however fubverfive of virtue they may be in theory,
there is fome *falvo* for good morals; fo
that, in fact, they enforce the more effential parts, at leaft, of that conduct,
which the good order of fociety requires.
Befides, it might be expected, that if all
the modes of religion were equally protected by the civil magiftrate, they would
all vie with one another, which fhould
best

beft deferve that protection. This, however, is, in fact, all the alliance that can take place between religion and civil policy, each enforcing the fame conduct by different motives. Any other *alliance between church and ftate* is only the alliance of different forts of worldly minded men, for their temporal emolument.

If I be urged with the horrid exceffes of the anabaptifts in Germany, about the time of the reformation; of the Levellers in England, during the civil wars; and the fhocking practices of that people in Afia, from whom we borrow the term *affaffin*; I anfwer, that, befides its being abfolutely chimerical to apprehend any fuch extravagances at prefent, and that they can never fubfift long; fuch outrages as thefe, againft the peace of fociety, may be reftrained by the civil magiftrate, without his troubling himfelf about religious opinions. If a man commit murder, let him be punifhed as a

mur-

murderer, and let no regard be paid to his plea of confcience for committing the action; but let not the opinions, which lead to the action be meddled with: for then, it is probable, that more harm will be done than good, and, that for a fmall evident advantage, rifque will be run of endlefs and unknown evils; or if the civil magiftrate never interfere in religion but in fuch cafes as thofe before mentioned, the friends of liberty will have no great reafon to complain. Confidering what great encroachments have been made upon their rights in feveral countries of Europe, they will be fatisfied if *part of the load* be removed. They will fupport themfelves with the hope, that, as the ftate will certainly find a folid advantage in every relaxation of its claim upon men's confciences, it will relax more and more of its pretended rights; till, at laft, religious opinions, and religious actions, be as free as the air we breathe, or the light of the common fun.

Eccle-

Ecclefiaftical authority may have been neceffary in the infant ftate of fociety ; and, for the fame reafon, it may, perhaps, continue to be, in fome degree, neceffary as long as fociety is imperfect ; and therefore may not be entirely abolifhed, till civil government have arrived at a much greater degree of perfection.

If, therefore, I were asked, whether I fhould approve of the immediate diffolution of all the ecclefiaftical eftablifhments in Europe, I fhould anfwer, no. This might, poffibly, efpecially in fome countries, for reafons that cannot be forefeen, be too hazardous an experiment. To begin with due caution, let experiments be firft made of *alterations*; or, which is the fame thing, of *better eftablifhments* than the prefent. Let them be reformed in many effential articles, and then not thrown afide entirely, till it be found by experience, that no good can be made of them. If I be

I   asked

asked in what particulars I imagine them to be moſt deficient, and what *kind* of reformation I could wiſh to have made in them; I anſwer, I could wiſh they were reformed in the four following reſpeɗs, which are all of a capital nature, and in which almoſt all our preſent eſtabliſhments are fundamentally wrong; as I make no doubt will appear to every man, of common ſenſe, who ſhall give the leaſt attention to this ſubjeɗ.

1. Let the articles of faith, to be ſubſcribed by candidates for the miniſtry, be greatly reduced. In the formulary of the church of England, might not thirty-eight out of the thirty-nine be very well ſpared? It is a reproach to any chriſtian eſtabliſhment, if every man cannot claim the benefit of it, who can ſay, that he believes in the religion of *Jeſus Chriſt*, as it is ſet forth in the *New Teſtament*. You ſay the terms are ſo general, that even deiſts would quibble, and inſinuate themſelves. I anſwer, that
all

all the articles which are fubfcribed at prefent, by no means exclude deifts who will prevaricate; and upon this fcheme you would at leaft exclude fewer honeft men. But all temptation to prevaricate will be taken away if the next article of reformation be attended to.

2. Let the livings of the clergy be made more equal, in proportion to the duty required of each : and when the ftipend is fettled, let not the importance of the office be eftimated above its real value. Let nothing be confidered but the work, and the neceffary expences of a liberal education.

3. Let the clergy be confined to their ecclefiaftical duty, and have nothing to do in conducting affairs of ftate. Is not their prefence in the cabinet rather dangerous ? The feat of our bifhops in parliament is a relick of the popifh ufurpations over the temporal rights of the fovereigns of Europe; and is not every

thing

thing of this nature juftly confidered as a great abfurdity in modern government? The queftion, by what right they fit, need not be difcuffed. As teachers of the religion of Chrift, whofe kingdom was not of this world, can they have any bufinefs to meddle with civil government? However, if they be allowed to fit in the great council of the nation, as members of the community at large; fuppofe they were fairly elected like other members; but fhould fuch a civil power as they now have devolve upon them, as a matter of courfe, on any pretence whatever?

4. Let the fyftem of *toleration* be completely carried into execution: and let every member of the community enjoy every right of a citizen, whether he chufe to conform to the eftablifhed religion or not. Let every man, who has fufficient abilities, be deemed qualified to ferve his country in any civil capacity. Becaufe a man cannot be a
bifhop,

bifhop, muft he therefore be nothing in
the ftate, and his country derive no benefit from his talents ? Befides, let it be
confidered, that thofe who depart the
fartheft from eftablifhed opinions will
have more at ftake in a country where
they enjoy thefe fingular privileges ;
and; confequently, will be more attached to it.

The toleration in England, notwithftanding our boafted liberty, is far from
being complete. Our prefent laws do
not tolerate thofe more rational diffenters, whom the bifhop of Gloucefter
looks upon as brethren. It is known to
every body, that if the toleration act was
ftrictly put in execution, it would filence
all thefe diffenting minifters who are held
in any degree of efteem by the church ;
in the fame manner as a truly confcientious fubfcription to the thirty nine articles would filence almoft all that are
rational, and free from enthufiafm, among
themfelves. It is not the law, but the

mild-

mildnefs of the adminiftration, and the fpirit of the times to which we are in-debted for our prefent liberties. But the man who fhould attempt to abufe the letter of the law, contrary to the fpirit of the times, and in order to trample upon the facred rights of humanity, will ever be infamous.

It will be faid, that a regard to liberty itfelf muft plead for one exception to the principles of toleration. The papifts, it is alledged, are fuch determined enemies to liberty, civil and ecclefiaftical, and fo effectually alienated from the interefts of a proteftant country and government, that proteftants, who have a regard for their own fafety, and the great caufe in which they are engaged, cannot tolerate them. If they do it, it is at their own peril; fo that the perfecution of papifts is, in fact, nothing more than a dictate of felf-prefervation.

This

This plea, I own, is plaufible; and two centuries ago it is no wonder it had confiderable weight; but perfecution by *proteftants*, in this enlightened age, appears fo utterly repugnant to the great principle of their caufe, that I wifh they would view it in every point of light, before they ferioufly adopt any fuch meafure. And I cannot help thinking, that the refult of a more mature confideration of this fubject will not be to *render evil for evil* to our old mother church, but rather a more indulgent treatment than we have as yet vouchfafed to afford her.

In the firft place, I cannot imagine that the increafe of popery, in thefe kingdoms, will ever be fo confiderable, as to give any juft alarm to the friends of liberty. All the addrefs and affiduity of man cannot, certainly, recommend fo abfurd a fyftem of faith and practice to any but the loweft and moft illiterate of our common people, who can never

I 4   have

have any degree of influence in the state. The number of popish gentry must grow less; partly through the influence of fashion, and partly through the conviction of those who may have a liberal education, which will necessarily throw protestant books into their hands.

If the popish priests and missionaries have the success which it is pretended they have, I am almost persuaded, that the most effectual arguments they have employed for this purpose, have been drawn from the rigour of our present laws respecting the papists. They tell the people, that, conscious of the weakness of our cause, we dare not give them full liberty to teach and exercise their religion; knowing that the excellency of it is such, that, if it were publicly exhibited, it would attract universal admiration; and that what we are not able to silence by argument, we suppress by force.

Besides,

Befides, the traces and remains of popery are fo ftriking in the book of common prayer, and in the whole fyftem of our ecclefiaftical eftablifhment, that the derivation of it from the popifh fyftem cannot be concealed ; and hence it may not be difficult for an artful papift, to perfuade many of the common people to quit the fhadow, and have recourfe to the fubftance ; to abandon the interefts of an apoftate child, and adopt that of its ancient and venerable parent.

Let the church of England then, before it be too late, make a farther reformation from popery, and leave fewer of the fymbols of the Romifh church about her : and the ideas of her members being more remote from every thing that has any connection with popery, the popifh miffionaries will have much more difficulty in making them comprehend and relifh it. A convert to popery from any of the fects of proteftant diffen-

ters,

ters (who are farther removed from the
popifh fyftem than the church of England) was, I believe, never heard of. And
this effect is not owing to any particular
care of their minifters to guard their
hearers againft popery; but becaufe the
whole fyftem of their faith and practice
is fo contrary to it, that even the common people, among them, would as foon
turn mahometans, or pagans, as become
papifts.

Inftead, then, of ufing more rigour
with the papifts, let us allow them a full
toleration. We fhould, at leaft, by this
means, be better judges of their number, and encreafe. And I alfo think
they would be much lefs formidable in
thefe circumftances, than they are at
prefent. If they be enemies, an open
enemy is lefs dangerous than a fecret one.
And if our ecclefiaftical eftablifhment
muft not be reformed, and removed farther from popery; let the clergy, as the
beft *fuccedaneum* for fuch an effectual
antidote

antidote againſt their poiſon, ſhow more zeal in the diſcharge of their parochial duties, and give more attention to their flocks. Half the zeal which the papiſts employ, to make converts, would be more than ſufficient to prevent any from being made: and whoſe buſineſs is it to counteract the endeavours of the popiſh emiſſaries, but thoſe whom the ſtate has appointed the guardians of the people in ſpiritual matters? And what is their calling in the aid of the civil power, but an acknowledgement of a neglect of their proper duty?

It may be ſaid, that the particular ſituation of this country ſhould be a motive with all the friends of our happy conſtitution, to keep a watchful eye over the papiſts; ſince a popiſh religion may, at length, fix a popiſh pretender upon the throne of theſe kingdoms. Seriouſly as this argument for perſecution might have been urged formerly, I cannot help thinking that, ever ſince the laſt rebellion,

the

the apprehenfion on which it is grounded, is become abfolutely chimerical, and therefore that it does not deferve a ferious anfwer; fo that the pretence will now be confidered to be as poor, as the caufe it is defigned to fubferve is bad. After the pope himfelf has refufed to acknowledge the heir of the Stuart family to be king of England, what can a papift, as fuch, have to plead for him? And, for my own part, I make no doubt, there are men of good fenfe among the popifh gentry, at leaft, and perfons of property of that perfuafion, as well as among perfons of other religious profeffions; and therefore, that if they laid under fewer civil difadvantages, they would not only chearfully acquiefce in, but would become zealoufly attached to our excellent form of *free government*; and that, upon any emergency, they would bravely ftand up for it, proteftant as it is, in oppofition to any popifh fyftem of *arbitrary power* whatever.

Befides,

Befides, when a popifh country is at this very time, fhowing us an example of a toleration, more perfect, in feveral refpects, than any which the church of England allows to thofe who diffent from her, is it not time to advance a little farther? Political confiderations may juftly be allowed to have fome weight in this cafe. France may reafonably be expected to follow, and improve upon the example of Poland; and if we do not make fome fpeedy improvement of liberty, that great and indefatigable rival power, by one mafter ftroke of policy, may almoft depopulate this great and flourifhing kingdom.

We often hear it faid, that if France grows wife, and admits of toleration, England is undone. Novelty, and a milder climate, will, no doubt, attract multitudes; and whenever the French make a reformation, as their minds are much more enlightened, than thofe of the Englifh reformers were, when our

prefent

prefent eftablifhment was fixed, their reformation will, in all probability, be much more perfect than ours. And if the French through our folly, and the ambition, avarice, or bafenefs of fome fpiritual dignitaries, fhould be permitted to take the lead in this noble work, and our emulation be not roufed by their example, the future motto of England may, with too much propriety, be taken from Bacon's fpeaking ftatue, TIME IS PAST.

PART

P A R T III.

Of the Progress of Civil Societies to a State of greater Perfection, showing that it is retarded by Encroachments on Civil and Religious Liberty.

THE great argument in favour of the perpetuation of ecclesiastical establishments is, that, as they suit the several forms of civil government under which they have taken place, the one cannot be touched without endangering the other. I am not insensible of the truth there is in the principle on which this apprehension is grounded; but I think the connection, artfully as those things have been interwoven, is not so strict, but that they may be separated, at least, in a course of time. But allowing that some change might take place in our

civil

civil conftitution, in confequence of the abolition or reformation of the ecclefiaftical part, it is more than an equal chance, that the alteration will be for the better; and no real friend to his country can wifh to perpetuate its prefent conftitution in church or ftate, fo far as to interrupt its progrefs to greater perfection than it has yet attained to.

I can heartily join with the greateft admirers of the Englifh conftitution, in their encomiums upon it, when it is compared with that of any other country in the world. I really think it to be the beft actual fcheme of civil policy; but if any perfon fhould fay, that it is perfect, and that no alteration can be made in it for the better, I beg leave to withhold my affent. Dr. Brown himfelf doth not hefitate to acknowledge, that there are imperfections in it. How then can a real friend to his country wifh to fix its imperfections upon it, and make them perpetual?

It

It will be faid, that alterations may, indeed, be made, but cannot be made with fafety, and without the danger of throwing every thing into confufion; fo that, upon the whole, things had better remain as they are : but, allowing this, for the prefent, why fhould they be perpetuated as they are ? If the propofed alterations were violent ones, that is, introduced by violent meafures, they might juftly give alarm to all good citizens. I would endeavour to ftop the ableft hand that fhould attempt to reform in this manner; becaufe it is hardly poffible but that a remedy fo effected muft be worfe than the difeafe. But ftill, why fhould we object to any ftate's gradually reforming itfelf, or throw obftacles in the way of fuch reformations.

All civil focieties, and the whole fcience of civil government on which they are founded, are yet in their infancy. Like other arts and fciences, this is gradually

K   improv-

improving; but it improves more flowly, becaufe opportunities for making experiments are fewer. Indeed, hardly any trials in legiflation have ever been made by perfons who had knowledge and ability to collect from hiftory, and to compare the obfervations which might be of ufe for this purpofe, or had leifure to digeft them properly at the time. Taking it for granted, therefore, that our conftitution and laws have not efcaped the imperfections which we fee to be incident to every thing human; by all means, let the clofeft attention be given to them, let their excellencies and defects be thoroughly laid open, and let improvements of every kind be made; but not fuch as would prevent all further improvements: becaufe it is not probable, that any improvements, which the utmoft fagacity of man could now fuggeft, would be an equivalent for the prevention of all that might be made hereafter. Were the beft formed ftate in the world to be fixed in its prefent condition, I make no doubt but

but that, in a courfe of time, it would be the worft.

Hiftory demonftrates this truth with refpect to all the celebrated ftates of antiquity; and as all things (and particularly whatever depends upon fcience) have of late years been in a quicker progrefs towards perfection than ever; we may fafely conclude the fame with refpect to any political ftate now in being. What advantage did Sparta (the conftitution of whofe government was fo much admired by the ancients, and many moderns) reap from thofe inftitutions which contributed to its longevity, but the longer continuance of, what I fhould not fcruple to call, the worft government we read of in the world; a government which fecured to a man the feweft of his natural rights, and of which a man who had a tafte for life would leaft of all chufe to be a member. While the arts of life were improving in all the neighbouring nations, Sparta derived this noble prerogative from her conftitu-

K 2   tion,

tion, that she continued the nearest to her pristine barbarity; and in the space of near a thousand years (which includes the whole period in which letters and the arts were the most cultivated in the rest of Greece) produced no one poet, orator, historian, or artist of any kind. The convulsions of Athens, where life was in some measure enjoyed, and the faculties of body and mind had their proper exercise and gratification, were, in my opinion, far preferable to the savage uniformity of Sparta.

The constitution of Egypt was similar to that of Sparta, and the advantages that country received from it were similar. Egypt was the mother of the arts to the states of Greece : but the rigid institutions of this mother of the arts kept them in their infancy; so that the states of Greece, being more favourably situated for improvements of all kinds, soon went beyond their instructress ; while no improvements of any kind were ever made

in

in Egypt, till it was fubdued by a foreign power. What would have been
the ftate of agriculture, fhip-building, or
war, if thofe arts had been fixed in England two or three centuries ago?

Dr. Brown will urge me with the authority of Plutarch, who largely extols
the regulations of Egypt and of Sparta,
and cenfures the Roman legiflators for
adopting nothing fimilar to them. But
I beg leave to appeal from the authority
of Plutarch, and of all the ancients, as by
no means competent judges in this cafe.
Imperfect as the fcience of government
is at prefent, it is certainly much more
perfect than it was in their time. On
the authority of the ancients, Dr. Brown
might as well contend for another inftitution of the famed Egyptians; viz. their
obliging all perfons to follow the occu-
pations of their fathers; and perhaps this
might be no bad auxiliary to his prefcribed mode of education, and prevent
the fpringing up of faction in a ftate. It

would

would likewife favour another object, which the doctor has profeffedly in view, viz. checking the growth of commerce.

Suppofing this wife fyftem of perpetuation had occured to our anceftors in the feudal times, and that an affembly of old Englifh barons, with their heads full of their feudal rights and fervices, had imitated the wife Spartans, and perpetuated the fevere feudal inftitutions; what would England at this day have been (with the unrivalled reputation of uniformity and conftancy in its laws) but the moft barbarous, the weakeft, and moft diftracted ftate in Europe? It is plain from fact, that divine providence had greater things in view in favour of thefe kingdoms; and has been conducting them through a feries of gradual changes (arifing from internal aud external caufes) which have brought us to our prefent happy condition; and which, if fuffered to go on, will probably carry us to a pitch of happinefs

nefs of which we can yet form no con-
ception.

Had the religious fyftem of our oldeft
forefathers been eftablifhed on thefe wife
and perpetual foundations, we had now
been pagans, and our priefts druids.
Had our Saxon conquerors been endued
with the fame wifdom and forefight, we
had been worfhipping Thor and Woden;
and had our anceftors, three centuries
ago, perfevered in this fpirit, we had
been blind and prieft-ridden papifts.
The greateft blefling that can befall a
ftate, which is fo rigid and inflexible
in its inftitutions, is to be conquered by
a people, who have a better government, and have made farther advances
in the arts of life. And it is undoubtedly a great advantage which the divine
being has provided for this world, that
conquefts and revolutions fhould give
mankind an opportunity of reforming
their fyftems of government, and of im-

K 4   proving

proving the science of it, which they would never have found themselves.

In the excellent constitution of nature, evils of all kinds, some way or other, find their proper remedy ; and when government, religion, education, and every thing that is valuable in society seems to be in so fine a progress towards a more perfect state, is it not our wisdom to favour this progress ; and to allow the remedies of all disorders to operate gradually and easily, rather than, by a violent system of perpetuation, to retain all disorders till they force a remedy ? In the excellent constitution of the human body, a variety of outlets are provided for noxious humours, by means of which the system relieves itself when any slight disorders happen to it. But, if these outlets be obstructed, the whole system is endangered by the convulsions which ensue.

Some

Some things in civil fociety do, in their own nature, require to be efta-blifhed, or fixed by law for a confider-able time : but that part of the fyftem, for the reafons mentioned above, will certainly be the moft imperfect ; and therefore it is the wifdom of the legifla-ture to make that part as fmall as poffi-ble, and to let the eftablifhments, which are neceffary, be as eafy as is confiftent with the tolerable order of fociety. It is an univerfal maxim, that the more liberty is given to every thing which is in a ftate of growth, the more perfect it will become ; and when it is grown to its full fize, the more amply will it repay its wife parent, for the indulgence given to it in its infant ftate. A judicious father will bear with the frowardnefs of his children, and overlook many flights of youth ; which can give him no plea-fure, but from the profpect they afford of his children becoming ufeful and va-luable men, when the fire of youth is abated.

I do

I do not pretend to define what degree of eftablifhment is neceffary for religion, or for many other articles in civil fociety: but it feems very clear that education requires none. And thus much I think is alfo clear, that every fyftem of policy is too ftrict and violent, in which any thing that may be the inftrument of general happinefs, is under fo much reftraint, that it can never reform itfelf from the diforders which may be incident to it; when it is fo circumftanced, that it cannot improve as far as it is capable of improvement, but that every reformation muft neceffarily be introduced from fome other quarter; in which cafe it muft generally be brought about by force. Is it not a ftanding argument that religion, in particular, has been too much confined, in all countries, that the body of the clergy have never reformed themfelves; and that all reformations have ever been forced upon them, and have generally been attended with the moft horrible

per-

perfecutions, and dangerous convulfions in the ftate ? I cannot help thinking alfo, that every fyftem of government is violent and tyrannical, which incapacitates men of the beft abilities, and of the greateft integrity, from rendering their country any fervice in their power, while thofe who pay no regard to confcience may have free accefs to all places of power and profit.

It feems to be the uniform intention of divine providence, to lead mankind to happinefs in a progreffive, which is the fureft, though the floweft method. Evil always leads to good, and imperfect to perfect. The divine being might, no doubt, have adopted a different plan, have made human nature and human governments perfect from the beginning. He might have formed the human mind with an intuitive knowledge of truth, without leading men through fo many labyrinths of error. He might have made man perfectly virtuous, without

giving

giving fo much exercife to his paffions
in his ftruggles with the habits of vice.
He might have fent an angel, or have
commiffioned a man to eftablifh a perfect form of civil government ; and,
a priori, this would feem to have been
almoft as effential to human happinefs as any fyftem of truth ; at leaft,
that it would have been a valuable ad-
dition to a fyftem of religious truth:
but though it would be impiety in us
to pretend to fathom the depths of the
divine councils, I think we may fairly
conclude, that if this method of proceeding had been the beft for us, he,
whom we cannot conceive to be influenced by any thing but his defire to promote the happinefs of his creatures,
would have purfued it. But a contrary
method has been adopted in every thing
relating to us.

How many falls does a child get before it learns to walk fecure. How many
inarticulate founds precede thofe which
are

are articulate. How often are we impofed upon by all our fenfes before we
learn to form a right judgment of the
proper objects of them. How often do
our paffions miflead us, and involve us
in difficulties, before we reap the advantage they were intended to bring us
in our purfuit of happinefs; and how
many falfe judgments do we make, in
the inveftigation of all kinds of truth,
before we come to a right conclufion.
How many ages do errors and prejudices
of all kinds prevail, before they are diffipated by the light of truth, and how
general, and how long was the reign of
falfe religion before the propagation of
the true! How late was chriftianity,
that great remedy of vice and ignorance,
introduced! How flow and how confined
its progrefs!

In fhort, it feems to have been the intention of divine providence, that mankind fhould be, as far as poffible, felf
taught; that we fhould attain to every
                                        thing

thing excellent and ufeful, as the refult of our own experience and obfervation ; that our. judgments fhould be formed by the appearances which are prefented to them, and our hearts inftructed by their own feelings. But by the unnatural fyftem of rigid unalterable eftablifhments, we put it out of our power to inftruct ourfelves, or to derive any advantage from the lights we acquire from experience and obfervation ; and thereby, as far as is in our power, we counteract the kind intentions of the deity in the conftitution of the world, and in providing for a ftate of conftant, though flow improvement in every thing.

A variety of ufeful leffons may be learned from our attention to the conduct of divine providence refpecting us. When hiftory and experience demonftrate the uniform method of divine providence to have been what has been above reprefented, let us learn from it
to

to be content with the natural, though
flow progrefs we are in to a more perfect
ftate. But let us always endeavour to
keep things in this progrefs. Let us,
however, beware, left by attempting to
accelerate, we in fact retard our progrefs
in happinefs. But more efpecially, let
us take heed, left, by endeavouring to
fecure and perpetuate the great ends of
fociety, we in fact defeat thofe ends.
We fhall have a thoufand times more
enjoyment of a happy and perfect form
of government, when we can fee in
hiftory the long progrefs of our conftitution through barbarous and imperfect
fyftems of policy; as we are more con-
firmed in the truth, and have more enjoyment of it, by reviewing the many
errors by which we were mifled in our
purfuit of it. If the divine being faw
that the beft form of government, that
even he could have prefcribed for us,
would not have anfwered the end of its
inftitution, if it had been impofed by
himfelf ; much lefs can we imagine it
could

could anfwer any valuable purpofe, to have the crude fyftems (for they can be nothing more) of fhort-fighted men for ever impofed upon us.

Eftablifhments, be they ever fo excellent, ftill fix things fomewhere; and this circumftance, which is all that is pleaded for them amounts to, is with me the greateft objection to them. I wifh to fee things *in a progrefs* to a better ftate, and no obftructions thrown in the way of reformation.

In fpite of all the fetters we can lay upon the human mind, notwithftanding all poffible difcouragements in the way of free inquiry, knowledge of all kinds, and religious knowledge among the reft, will increafe. The wifdom of one generation will ever be folly in the next. And yet, though we have feen this verified in the hiftory of near two thoufand years, we perfift in the abfurd maxim of making a preceding generation dictate

dictate to a fucceeding one, which is
the fame thing as making the foolifh inftruct the wife; for what is a lower
degree of wifdom but comparative folly?

Had even Locke, Clarke, Hoadly, and
others, who have gained immortal reputation by their freedom of thinking, but
about half a century ago, been appointed to draw up a creed, they fhould
have inferted in it fuch articles of faith,
as myfelf, and hundreds more, would
now think unfcriptural, and abfurd:
nay, articles, which they would have
thought of great importance, we fhould
think conveyed a reflection upon the
moral government of God, and were in-
jurious to virtue among men. And can we
think that wifdom will die with us! no,
our creeds; could we be fo inconfiftant
with ourfelves as to draw up any, would,
I make no doubt, be rejected with equal
difdain by our pofterity.

L   That

That ecclefiaftical eftablifhments have really retarded the reformation from popery is evident from the face of things in Europe. Can it be thought that all the errors and abufes which had been accumulating in the fpace of fifteen hundred years, fhould be rectified in lefs than fifty, by men educated with ftrong prejudices in favour of them all? and yet the Augsburg confeffion, I believe, ftands unrepealed; the church of England is the fame now that it was in the reign of Queen Elizabeth; and the church of Scotland is to this day in that imperfect and crude ftate in which *John Knox* left it.

Little did thofe great reformers, whofe memory I revere, think what burdens they, who had boldly fhaken off the load from their own fhoulders, were laying on thofe of others; and that the moment they had nobly freed themfelves from the yoke of fervitude, they were figning an act to enflave all that fhould come after them;

them ; forgetting the golden rule of the gofpel, to do to others as we would that they fhould do to us.

Could religious knowledge have re-mained in the ftate in which the firft reformers left it ; could the ftone they had once moved from its feat, on the top of a precipice, have been ftopped in its courfe, their provifions for perpetuation would have been wife and excellent ; but their eyes were hardly clofed, before their children found that their fathers had been too precipitate. They found their own hands tied up by their un-thinking parents, and the knots too many, and too tight for them to un-loofe.

The great misfortune is, that the progrefs of knowledge is chiefly among the thinking few. The bulk of man-kind, being educated in a reverence for eftablifhed modes of thinking and acting, in confequence of their being eftablifhed,

will

will not hear of a reformation proceeding even fo far as they could really wifh, left, in time, it fhould go farther than they could wifh, and the end be worfe than the beginning. And where there are great emoluments in a church, it is poffeffed of the ftrongeft internal guard againft all innovations whatever. Church livings muft not be touched, and they may, if any thing elfe be meddled with. This makes the fituation of fenfible and confcientious men, in all eftablifhments, truly deplorable. Before I had read that excellent work, intitled the *Confeffional*, but much more fince, it has grieved me to fee the miferable fhifts that fuch perfons (whether in the church of England, or of Scotland) are obliged to have recourfe to, in order to gild the pill, which they muft fwallow or ftarve ; and to obferve their poor contrivances to conceal the chains that gall them. But it grieves one no lefs, to fee the reft of their brethren, hugging their chains and proud of them.

But

But let thofe gentlemen in the church, who oppofe every ftep towards reformation, take care, left they overact their parts, and left fome enterprizing perfons, finding themfelves unable to untie the Gordian knots of authority, fhould, like another Alexander the Great, boldly cut them all. Let them take care, left, for want of permitting a few repairs in their ruinous houfe, it fhould at laft fall all together about their ears. A number of fpirited and confcientious men, openly refufing to enter into the church, or throwing up the livings which they hold upon thofe iniquitous and enflaving terms (and fuch men there have been in this country) would roufe the attention of the temporal heads of our fpiritual church. They might fee the neceffity of an immediate and compleat reformation; and the alarm of churchmen, with their paultry expedients and compromifes, would come too late. The temper of thefe times would not bear a fecond St. Bartholomew.

In the mean time, let the friends of liberty by no means give way to impatience. The longer it be before this reformation takes place, the more effectual it will probably be. The times may not yet be ripe for such an one as you would wifh to acquiefce in, confidering that, whenever it is made, it will probably continue as long as the laft has done.

It was well for the caufe of truth and liberty, that the Romifh clergy at the firft beginning of the reformation, held out with fo much obftinacy againft the fmalleft conceffions; for had they but granted the cup to the laity, and been a little more decent in the article of indulgences, the reft of popery might have continued

" To fcourge mankind for ten dark ages more."

And at the reftoration here in England, had a few, a very few trifling alterations been complied with, fuch numbers of
the

the prefbyterians would have heartily united to the eftablifhed church, as
would have enabled it entirely to crufh
every other fect, to prevent the growing
liberty of the prefs, and to have maintained for ages the moft rigid uniformity. This obfervation may, perhaps,
teach patience to one party, and pru-
dence to the other.

Diffenters, even of the prefbyterian
perfuafion, have, by no means, been
free from the general infatuation of all
other reformers. All the denominations
of diffenters have made attempts to fix
things by their own narrow ftandard;
and prefcribed confeffions of faith, even
with fubfcriptions, have been introduced among them. But happily for us,
there have always been men of generous
and enlarged minds, who, having no civil
power to contend with, have had courage to ftem the torrent; and now,
among thofe who are called the more
rational part of the diffenters, things are

not,

not, upon the whole, to be complained of
No fubfcriptions to any articles of faith,
or even to the new teftament, is now
required ; and minifters are excufed, if
they chufe not to give any confeffion of
their own. To have preached and be-
haved like a chriftian, is deemed fufficient to recommend a man to the chriftian miniftry. Unfettered by authority,
they can purfue the moft liberal plans
of education. The whole bufinefs is
to give the faculties of the mind their
free play, and to point out proper objects of attention to ftudents, without
any concern what may be the refult of
their inquiries ; the bufinefs being to
make wife and ufeful men, and not the
tools and abettcrs of any particular
party.

If any perfon fhould think that religion is not to be put upon the fame footing with other branches of knowledge
(which they allow to require the aid of
every circumftance favourable to their
future

future growth) that fince the whole of chriftianity was delivered at once, and is contained in the books of the new teftament, there is no reafon to expect more light than we already have with regard to it; and, therefore, that they are juftified in fixing the knowledge of it where it *now* ftands, I fhall only fay, that I fincerely pity their weaknefs and prejudice; as fuch an opinion can only proceed from a total ignorance of what has paffed in the chriftian world, or from a bigotted attachment to the authorita-tive inftitutions of falliable men.

To recur to Dr. Brown : he would raife the terms on which we are to live in fo-ciety; fo that, under his adminiftration, a man could enjoy little more than bare fecurity in the poffeffion of his property, and that upon very hard conditions. The care he would take to fhackle men's minds, in the firft formation of their thinking powers, and to check their exertions when they were formed, would,

I ap-

I apprehend, put an effectual ftop to all the noble improvements of which fociety is capable. Knowledge, particularly of the more fublime kinds, in the fciences of morals and religion, could expect no encouragement. He would have more reftrictions laid upon the publication of books. He complains, page 103, that, in the late reign, deiftical publications proceeded almoft without cognifance from the civil magiftrate; and afferts, Appendix, page 29, that there are *many* opinions or principles tending evidently to the deftruction of fociety or freedom, and which, therefore, ought not to be tolerated in a well ordered free community.

The civil magiftrate then, according to this writer, ought to control the prefs, and therefore prevent, by means of effectual penalties (or elfe he doth nothing) the publication of any thing, that might directly or indirectly, thwart his views of civil policy; which, in England,

England, comprehends the prefent form of our eftablifhed religion. But fo extenfive is the connection of all kinds of truth, that if a man would keep effectually clear of the fubject of religion, he muft not indulge a free range of thought near the confines of it. The fubjects of metaphyfics, morals, and natural religion would be highly dangerous. There might be herefy, or the foundation of herefy, without coming near revelation, or any of the peculiar doctrines of chriftianity. We muft only be allowed to *think* for ourfelves, without having the liberty of divulging, or, in any form, publifhing our thoughts to others, not even to our children. A mighty privilege indeed! and for which we might think ourfelves obliged to Dr. Brown, if it were in the power of man to deprive us of it. This is a privilege which the poor wretch enjoys who lives under the fame roof with a Spanifh inquifitor. The fubjects of the grand feignior enjoy far greater privileges

leges than thofe which Dr. Brown would indulge to Englifhmen. For the greater part of them are allowed to educate their children in a religion, which teaches them to regard Mohammed˙ as an impoftor. Nay, the pope himfelf permits thofe to live unmolefted, and under his protection at Rome, who look upon that church, of which he calls himfelf the head, as founded on fraud and falfehood, and to educate their children in the fame principles. Nor hath the pope, or the grand feignior, ever feen reafon to repent of their indulgence.

Were any more laws reftraining the liberty of the prefs in force, it is impof-fible to fay how far they might be con-ftrued to extend. Thofe already in be-ing are more than are requifite, and in-confiftent with the interefts of truth. Were they to extend farther, every au-thor would lie at the mercy of the mi-nifters of ftate, who might condemn in-difcriminately, upon fome pretence or other,

other, every work that gave them umbrage; under which circumſtances might
fall ſome of the greateſt and nobleſt productions of the human mind, if ſuch
works could be produced in thoſe circumſtances. For if men of genius
knew they could not publiſh the diſcoveries they made, they could not give
free ſcope to their faculties in making
and purſuing thoſe diſcoveries. It is the
thought of publication, and the pro-
ſpect of fame which is, generally, the
great incentive to men of genius to exert
their faculties, in attempting the untrod-
den paths of ſpeculation.

In thoſe unhappy circumſtances, writers would entertain a dread of every new
ſubject. No man could ſafely indulge
himſelf in any thing bold, enterprizing,
and out of the vulgar road; and in all
publications we ſhould ſee a timidity in-
compatible with the ſpirit of diſcovery.
If any towering genius ſhould ariſe in
thoſe unfavourable circumſtances, a
Newton

Newton in the natural world, or a Locke, a Hutchefon, a Clarke, or a Hartley in the moral, the only effectual method to prevent their diffufing a fpirit of enterprife and innovation, which is natural to fuch great fouls, could be no other than that which Tarquin fo fignificantly expreffed, by taking off the heads of all thofe poppies which overlooked the reft. Such men could not but be dangerous, and give umbrage in a country where it was the maxim of the government, that every thing of importance fhould for ever remain unalterably fixed.

The whole of this fyftem of uniformity appears to me to be founded on very narrow and fhort-fighted views of policy. A man of extenfive views will overlook temporary evils, with a profpect of the greater good which may often refult from, or be infeparably connected with them. He will bear with a few tares, left, in attempting to root them out, he endanger rooting up the wheat with them.

them. Unbounded free enquiry upon
all kinds of fubjects may certainly be attended with fome inconvenience, but it
cannot be reftrained without infinitely
greater inconvenience. The deiftical per-
formances Dr. Brown is fo much of-
fended at may have unfettled the minds
of fome people, but the minds of many
have been more firmly fettled, and upon
better foundations than ever. The
fcheme of chriftianity has been far better underftood, fince thofe deiftical writings have occafioned the fubject to be
more thoroughly difcuffed than it had
been before.

Befides, if truth ftand upon the falfe
foundation of prejudice or error, it is an
advantage to it to be unfettled; and the
man who doth no more, and even means
to do no more, is, in fact, its friend.
Another perfon feeing its deftitute and
bafelefs condition, may be induced to fet
it upon its proper foundation. Far better policy would it be to remove the difficulties

ficulties which ſtill lie in the way of
free enquiry, than to throw freſh ones
into it.   Infidels would then be deprived
of their moſt ſuccefsful method of at-
tacking chriſtianity, namely, infinuation;
and chriſtian divines might, with a more
manly grace, engage with the champi-
ons of deiſm, and in faċt engage with
more advantage, when they both fought
on the ſame equal ground.   As things
are at preſent, I ſhould be aſhamed to
fight under the ſhelter of the civil power,
while I ſaw my adverſary expoſed to all
the ſeverity of it.

To the ſame purpoſe, I cannot help
quoting the authority of Dr. Warburton,
" Nor lefs friendly is this liberty to the
" generous advocate of religion.   For
" how could ſuch an one, when in earneſt
" convinced of the ſtrength of evidence
" in his cauſe, defire an adverſary whom
" the laws had before diſarmed, or value
" a viċtory where the magiſtrate muſt
" triumph with him ? even I, the
                              " meaneſt

" meaneft in this controverfy, fhould have
" been afhamed of projecting the defence
" of the great Jewifh legiflator, did not I
" know, that his affailants and defenders
" fkirmifhed under one equal law of li-
" berty. And if my diffenting, in the
" courfe of this defence, from fome com-
" mon opinions needs an apology, I
" fhould defire it may be thought, that
" I ventured into this train with greater
" confidence, that I might fhew, by not
" intrenching myfelf in authorized fpe-
" culations, I put myfelf upon the fame
" footing with you [the deifts] and would
" claim no privilege that was not enjoy-
" ed in common." Divine Legation,
page 7.

But forry I am, that the paragraph
which immediately follows, how proper
foever it might be when it was written,
would *now* look like a tantalizing of his
unfortunate adverfaries. " This liberty,
" then, may you long poffefs, know
" how to ufe, and gratefully to acknow-

" ledge it. I fay this, becaufe one can-
" not, without indignation, obferve,
" that, amidft the full enjoyment of it,
" you ftill continue, with the meaneft
" affectation, to fill your prefaces with
" repeated clamours againft the difficul-
" ties and difcouragements attending the
" exercife of free thinking; and in a
" peculiar ftrain of modefty and reafon-
" ing, make ufe of this very liberty to
" perfuade the world you ftill want it.
" In extolling liberty we can join with
" you, in the vanity of pretending to
" have contributed moft to its eftablifh-
" ment we can bear with you, but in the
" low cunning of pretending ftill to lie
" under reftraints, we can neither join
" nor bear with you. There was, indeed,
" a time, and that within our memo-
" ries, when fuch complaints were fea-
" fonable, and meritorious; but, happy
" for you, gentlemen, you have outlived
" it. All the reft is merely fir Martin,
" it is continuing to fumble at the
" lute

" lute though the mufic has been long
" over."

Let Peter Annet (if he dare) write a
comment on this paffage. So far are
deifts from having free liberty to publifh
their fentiments, that even many chriftians cannot fpeak out with fafety. In
prefent circumftances, a chriftian divine
is not at liberty to make ufe of thofe
arguments which, he may think, would
fupply the beft defence of chriftianity.
What are, in the opinion of many, the
very foundations of our faith, are in a
ruinous condition, and muft be repaired
before it will be to any purpofe to beau-
tify and adorn the fuperftructure; but
the man who fhould have the true courage
and judgment, to go near enough to fuch
rotten foundations, would be thought to
mean nothing lefs than to undermine them,
and intirely deftroy the whole fabric. His
very brethren would ftand off from him,
think him in league with their adverfaries ;
and, by an ill judging zeal, might call
in the deftructive aid of the civil power

to ftop his hand. In confequence of which, notwithftanding his moft laudable zeal in favour of our holy religion, he might ftand upon the fame pillory, and be thrown into the fame prifon with wretched and harmlefs infidels. Many undoubted friends of chriftianity, and men of the moft enlarged minds, will know and feel what I mean.

Hitherto, indeed, few of the friends of free inquiry among chriftians have been more than partial advocates for it. If they find themfelves under any difficulty with refpect to their own fentiments, they complain, and plead ftrongly for the rights of confcience, of private judgment, and of free inquiry; but when they have gotten room enough for themfelves, they are quite eafy, and in no pain for others. The papift muft have liberty to write againft pagans, mohammedans, and jews; but he cannot bear with proteftants. Writers in defence of the church of England juftify
their

their feparation from the church of
Rome, but, with the moft glaring in-
confiftency, call the proteftant diffenters,
fchifmatics; and many diffenters, forgetting the fundamental principles of
their diffent, which are the fame that are
afferted by all chriftians and proteftants
in fimilar circumftances, difcourage every
degree of liberty greater than they themfelves have taken, and have as great an
averfion to thofe they are pleafed to call
heretics, as papifts have for proteftants,
or as Laud had for the old puritans.

But why fhould we confine our neighbour, who may want more room, in the
fame narrow limits with ourfelves. The
wider we make the common circle of
liberty, the more of its friends will it receive, and the ftronger will be the common intereft. Whatever be the particular views of the numerous tribes of
fearchers after truth, under whatever
denomination we may be ranked, whether we be called, or call ourfelves chri-

M 3   ftians

ftians, papifts, proteftants, diffenters, heretics, or even deifts (for all are equal
here, all are actuated by the fame fpirit,
and all engaged in the fame caufe) we
ftand in need of the fame liberty of thinking, debating, and publifhing. Let us,
then, as far as our intereft is the fame,
with one heart and voice, ftand up for it.
Not one of us can hurt his neighbour,
without ufing a weapon which, in the
hand of power, might as well ferve to
chaftife himfelf. The prefent ftate of
the Englifh government (including both
the laws, and the adminiftration, which
often corrects the rigour of the law) may,
perhaps, bear my own opinions without
taking much umbrage ; but I could wifh
to congratulate many of my brother free-
thinkers, on the greater indulgence which
their more heretical fentiments may require.

To the honour of the quakers be it
fpoken, that they are the only body of
chriftians who have uniformly maintained

tained the principles of chriftian liberty, and toleration. Every other body of men have turned perfecutors when they had power. Papifts have perfecuted the proteftants, the church of England has perfecuted the diffenters, and other diffenters in lofing their name, loft that fpirit of chriftian charity, which feemed to be effential to them: Short was their fun-fhine of power, and thankful may Britain, and the prefent diffenters be, that it was fo. But the quakers, though eftablifhed in Penfylvania, have perfecuted none. This glorious principle feems fo intimately connected with the fundamental maxims of their fect, that it may be fairly prefumed, the moderation they have hitherto fhown is not to be afcribed to the fmallnefs of their party, or to their fear of reprifals. For this reafon, if I were to pray for the general prevalence of any one fect of chriftians (which I fhould not think it for the intereft of chriftianity to take place, even though I fhould fettle the articles of it myfelf) it fhould be that of

M 4   the

the quakers; becaufe, different as my opinions are from theirs, I have fo much confidence in their moderation, that I believe they would let me live, write, and publifh what I pleafed unmolefted among them. And this I own, is more than I could promife myfelf from any other body of chriftians whatever; the prefbyterians by no means excepted.

The object of this forced uniformity is narrow and illiberal, unworthy of human nature. Suppofing it accomplifhed, what is it poffible to gain by it, but, perhaps, a more obftinate and blind belief in the vulgar; while men of fenfe, feeing themfelves debarred the very means of conviction, muft of courfe be infidels? In thofe circumftances, it would really be an argument of a man's want of fpirit, of fenfe, and even of virtue to be a believer, becaufe he would believe without fuffi-cient evidence. Who would not, with every appearance of juftice, fufpect any caufe, when he was not allowed to examine

mine the arguments againſt it, and was only preſſed with thoſe in its favour?

What ſenſible and upright judge would decide a cauſe, where all the witneſſes on one ſide were by violence prevented from giving their evidence? Thoſe who con-verſe with deiſts well know, that one of their ſtrongeſt objections to chriſtianity ariſes from hence, that none of the early writings againſt it are preſerved. How much ſtronger, and even unanſwerable, would that objection have been, if chriſ-tianity had been from the beginning, ſo effectually protected by the civil magi-ſtrate, that no perſon had dared to write againſt it at all. Such friends to the evi-dence and true intereſts of chriſtianity are all thoſe who would ſuppreſs deiſtical writings at this day!

Suppoſe any article in a ſyſtem of faith, ſo eſtabliſhed and guarded, to be wrong, which is certainly a very modeſt ſuppoſition; let any of the advocates of
this

this fcheme fay, how it is poffible it fhould ever be rectified ; or that if the truth fhould infinuate itfelf, by any avenue which they had not fufficiently guarded, how it could bring its evidence along with it, fo as to command the attention and acceptance which it deferved.

Indeed, it is not fo much from the miftaken friends of truth that we apprehend thefe meafures of rigid uniformity; but rather from thofe who would facrifice truth, and every other confideration to public tranquility. From thofe MERE STATESMEN who, looking upon all fyftems of religion to be equally falfe, and not able to bear examination, will not fuffer that examination to take place; for fear of deftroying a fyftem, which, however falfe, they imagine to be neceffary to the peace and well being of the ftate. The moft unrelenting perfecution is to be apprehended, not from bigots, but from infidels. A bigot, who is fo from a principle of confcience, may poffibly be moved by a regard to the confci-

confciences of others; but the man who thinks that confcience ought always to be facrificed to political views, has no principle on which an argument in favour of moderation can lay hold. Was not Bolingbroke the greateft promoter of the fchifm bill in England, and Richlieu of the perfecution of the proteftants in France?

I acknowledge with the ftatefman, that the proper object of the civil magiftrate is the peace and well being of fociety, and that whatever tends to difturb that peace and well being, properly comes under his cognifance. I acknowledge feveral religious and moral, as well as political principles have a near connection with the well being of fociety. But, as was more fully explained before, there are many cafes, in which the happinefs of fociety is nearly concerned, in which it would, neverthelefs, be the greateft impropriety for the civil magiftrate to interfere; as in many of the duties of private life, the obligations of gratitude,

gratitude, &c.   In all such cases, where the well being of society is most nearly concerned, the civil magistrate has no right to interfere, unless he can do it to good purpose.   There is no difference, I apprehend, to be made in this case, between the right, and the wisdom of interference.   If the interference would be for the good of the society upon the whole, it is wise, and right; if it would do more harm than good, it is foolish and wrong.   Let the sagacious statesman, therefore, consider, whether the interference of the civil magistrate be, in its own nature, calculated to prevent the violation of the religious and moral principles he may wish to enforce.   I think it is clear, that when they are in danger of being violated, his presence is so far from tending to remedy the evil, that it must necessarily inflame it, and make it worse.

It is universally understood, that REA-SON and AUTHORITY are two things, and
that

that they have generally been oppofed to one another; the hand of power, therefore, on the fide of any fet of principles cannot but be a fufpicious circumftance. And though the injunction of the magiftrate may filence *voices*, it multiplies *whifpers*; and thofe whifpers are the things at which he has the moft reafon to be alarmed.

Befides, it is univerfally true, that where the civil magiftrate has the greateft pretence for interfering in religious and moral principles, his interference (fuppofing there were no impropriety in it) is the leaft neceffary. If the opinions and principles in queftion, be evidently fubverfive of all religion and all civil fociety, they muft be evidently falfe, and eafy to refute; fo that there can be no danger of their fpreading; and the patrons of them may fafely be fuffered to maintain them in the moft open manner they chufe.

To

To mention thofe religious and moral principles which Dr. Brown produces, as the moft deftructive to the well being of fociety; namely, that *there is no God, and that there is no faith to be kept with heretics.* So far am I from being of his opinion, that it is neceffary to guard againft thefe principles by fevere penalties, and not to tolerate thofe who maintain them, that I think, of all opinions, furely fuch as thefe have nothing formidable or alarming in them. They can have no terrors but what the magiftrate himfelf, by his ill-judged oppofition, may give them. Perfecution may procure friends to any caufe, and poffibly to this, but hardly any thing elfe can do it. It is unqueftionable, that there are more atheifts and infidels of all kinds in Spain and Italy, where religion is fo well guarded, than in England; and it is, perhaps, principally owing to the laws in favour of chriftianity, that there are fo many deifts in this country.

For

For my own part, I cannot help thinking the principles of Dr. Brown very
dangerous in a free ſtate, and therefore
cannot but wiſh they were exterminated.
But I ſhould not think that ſilencing him
would be the beſt method of doing it.
No, let him, by all means, be encouraged
in making his ſentiments in public; both
that their dangerous tendency, and
their futility may more clearly appear.
Had I the direction of the preſs, he
ſhould be welcome to my *imprimatur* for
any thing he ſhould pleaſe to favour the
world with; and ready, if I know my-
ſelf, ſhould I be, to furniſh him with
every convenience in my power for that
purpoſe. It is for the intereſt of truth
that every thing be viewed in fair and
open day light, and it can only be ſome
ſiniſter purpoſe that is favoured by dark-
neſs or concealment of any kind. My
ſentiments may be fallacious, but if no
body were allowed to write againſt me,
how could that fallacy be made to appear

pear? be the prayer of the magnanimous Ajax ever mine,

Ποιησον δ' αιθρην, δος δ' οφθαλμοισιν ιδεσθαι·
Εν δι φαιι και ολισσον   Homer. Lib. 17. v. 646.

This writer artfully mentions only three opinions or principles, one under each clafs of religion, morals, and politics, as neceffary to be guarded by civil penalties, and not to be tolerated; and no doubt he has chofen thofe principles which a friend to his country would moft wifh to have fuppreffed, and with regard to which, he would leaft fcrupuloufly examine the means that might be ufed to fupprefs them. This, Britons, is the method in which arbitrary power has ever been introduced: this is well known to have been the method ufed by the thirty tyrants of Athens. They firft cut off perfons the moft generally obnoxious, and fuch as the ftanding laws could not reach. And even that intelligent people were fo far duped by their refent-

refentment, that they were not aware, that the very fame methods might be employed to take off the worthieft men in the city. And if ever arbitrary power fhould gain ground in England, it will be by means of the feeming neceflity of having recourfe to illegal methods, in order to come at opinions or perfons generally obnoxious. But when thefe illegal practices have once been authorized, and have paffed into precedents, all perfons and all opinions will lie at the mercy of the prime minifter, who will animadvert upon whatever gives him umbrage.

Happy would it be for the unfufpecting fons of liberty, if their enemies would fay, at firft, how far they meant to proceed againft them. To fay, as Dr. Brown does, that there are many opinions and principles which ought not to be tolerated, and to inftance only in three, is very fufpicious and alarming. Let him fay, in the name of all the

N   friends

friends of liberty, I challenge him or any of his friends to fay, how many more he has thought proper not to mention, and what they are; that we may not admit the foot of arbitrary power, before we fee what fize of a body the monfter has to follow it.

Such is the connection and gradation of opinions, that if once we admit there are *fome* which ought to be guarded by civil penalties, it will ever be impoffible to diftinguifh, to general fatisfaction, between thofe which may be tolerated, and thofe which may not. No two men living, were they queftioned ftrictly, would give the fame lift of fuch fundamentals. Far eafier were it to diftinguifh the exact boundaries of the animal, vegetable, and mineral kingdoms in nature, which yet naturalifts find to be impoffible. But a happy circumftance it is for human fociety, that, in religion and morals, there is no neceffity to diftinguifh them at all. The more im-

important will guard themfelves by their own evidence, and the lefs important do not deferve to be guarded.

Political principles, indeed, may require penal fanctions; but then it is for the very fame reafon that religious and moral principles require none. It is becaufe they do not carry their own evidence along with them. Governments actually eftablifhed muft guard themfelves by penalties and intolerance, becaufe forms of government, and perfons prefiding in them, being nearly arbitrary, it may not be very evident that a different government, or different governors, would not be better for a ftate. Laws relating to treafon are to be confidered as arifing from the principle of felf-prefervation. But even with refpect to civil government, it is better not to guard every thing fo ftrongly as that no alteration can ever be made in it. Nay, alterations are daily propofed, and daily take place in our civil government,

in

in things both of great and small confequence. They are improvements in
religion only that receive no countenance from the ftate : a fate fingular and
hard!

Befides, fo many are the fubtle dif-
tinctions relating to religion and morals,
that no magiftrate, or body of magiftrates, could be fuppofed to enter into
them; and yet, without entering into
them, no laws they could make would
be effectual. To inftance in the firft of
Dr. Brown's principles, and the moft
effential of them, viz. the being of a
God. The magiftrate muft define ftrictly what he means by the term God,
otherwife Epicureans and Spinozifts
might be no atheifts; or Arians or Atha-
nafians might be obnoxious to the law.
The magiftrate muft likewife punifh, not
only thofe who directly maintain the
principles of Atheifm (for evafions are
fo eafy to find, that fuch laws would
hurt no body) but he muft punifh thofe
who

who do it indirectly; and what opinions
are there not, in religion, morals, and
even natural philofophy, which might
not be faid to lead to Atheifm? The
doctrine of equivocal generation, for inftance, might certainly be thought of
this kind, as well as many others,
which have been very harmlefsly maintained by many good chriftians.

I am fenfible, that in the few particulars which Dr. Brown has thought
proper to mention, his intolerant principles are countenanced by Mr. Locke;
but, as far as I can recollect, thefe are
all the opinions which Locke would
not tolerate; whereas this writer afferts there are many; fo that he muft
provide himfelf with fome other authority for the reft. Befides I make
no doubt, the great Mr. Locke would,
without the leaft reluctance, have given
up any of his affertions, upon finding fo bad an ufe made of them, and
that the confequences of them were fo

N 3   very

very unfavourable to his own great object, and contradictory to his leading
principles; and that he would, with
indignation, have given up any adhe-
rents to arbitrary power, who, from
such a pretence as this, should claim
his protection from the generous pursuit of the friends of liberty, of rea-
son, and of mankind. And, after all,
the controversy is not about men, but
principles. And so great an enemy as
Mr. Locke to all authority in matters of opinion, would not have been so
inconsistent as to have excepted his own.

Besides, as was in some measure ob-
served before, all these systems of uniformity, in political or religious institutions, are the highest injustice to
posterity. What natural right have we
to judge for them, any more than
our ancestors had to judge for us?
our ancestors, from the time of the
Britons, had, no doubt, as high an opinion of their political and religious institutions

ftitutions as we can have of ours. But
fhould we not have thought the fate
of Great-Britain fingularly unhappy, if
they had been entailed upon us? and
the very fame reafon of complaint will
our pofterity have, if we take any methods to perpetuate what we approve,
as beft for ourfelves in our prefent
circumftances; for farther than this we
cannot pretend to fee.

Let us, by all means, make our own
circumftances as eafy as poffible; but let
us lay pofterity under no difficulty in
improving theirs, if they fee it con-
venient: rather, let all plans of policy
be fuch as will eafily admit of extenfion, and improvements of all kinds,
and that the leaft violence, or difficulty
of any kind, may attend the making
of them. This is, at leaft, very defirable, and I believe it is far from being impracticable. However, though it
fhould not be thought proper to unfix any
thing which is at prefent eftablifhed,

let

let us proceed no farther than is manifeftly neceffary in thofe eftablifhments.

I am not pleading againſt religious eftablifhments in all cafes; but only argue againſt fixing every thing ſo unalterably, that if a change, in any particular, ſhould be defired by a great majority of the clergy themſelves, they ſhould not be able to accomplifh it, without the danger of throwing every thing into confufion. Such rigid eftablifhments imply the authors of them to be well perfuaded of their own infallibility. For no man, who could ſuppofe it poffible for himſelf to be miſtaken, would think it was reafonable, that, after the miſtake was difcovered, and univerfally acknowledged to be a miſtake, all perfons (if they would enjoy the advantage of the eftablifhment) ſhould ever after be obliged to affirm, that they believed it to be no miſtake, but perfectly agreeable to truth.

How

How far this is the cafe with the church of England, let thofe of her clergy fay, who may underftand the fubject of religion a little better than the firft reformers, juft emerging from the darknefs of popery; who may have fome reluctance to fubfcribe what they do not believe, and who may feel, notwithftanding every evafion to which they can have recourfe, that a church preferment is dearly bought at the expence of a folemn falfehood. I do not appeal to thofe who may really believe all they fubfcribe, or to thofe who may fubfcribe without thinking at all, or to thofe who would wait upon any minifter of ftate in the world with a *carte blanche* ready figned. In faying this, I even hint no more than what many of the greateft ornaments of the church have faid again and again; that fome things, in our prefent eftablifhment, are wrong, and want reformation; and that there are thinking and unthinking, honeft and

difhoneft

difhoneft men in this, as well as in every other profeffion.

Pofterity, it may be faid, will never complain of our inftitutions, when they have been educated in a ftrong and invincible attachment to them. It is true; and had we been pagans or papifts, through a fimilar fyftem of education, fixed in a more early period, we fhould not have complained. We, like the old Spartans, or the fons of bigotry in Spain and Portugal at prefent, might have been hugging our chains, and even proud of them. But other perfons, who could have made a comparifon between our actual condition, and what it would have been, had thofe inftitutions not been made, would have complained for us. They would have feen us to be a lefs great, wife, and happy people; which affords the fame argument againft throwing difficulties in the way of future improvements.

Highly

Highly as we think of the wifdom of our anceftors, we juftly think ourfelves, of the prefent age, wifer, and, if we be not blinded by the mere prejudice of education, muft fee, that we can, in many refpects, improve upon the inftitutions they have tranfmitted to us. Let us not doubt, but that every generation in pofterity will be as much fuperior to us in political, and in all kinds of knowledge, and that they will be able to improve upon the beft civil and religious inftitutions that we can prefcribe for them. Inftead then of adding to the difficulties, which we ourfelves find in making the improvements we wifh to introduce, let us make this great and defirable work eafier to them than it has been to us.

However, fuch is the progrefs of knowledge, and the enlargement of the human mind, that, in future time, notwithftanding all poffible obftructions thrown in the way of human genius, men of great and exalted views will undoubtedly

doubtedly arife, who will fee through and deteft our narrow politics; when the ill-advifers and ill-advifed authors of thefe illiberal and contracted fchemes will be remembered with infamy and execration: when, notwithftanding their talents as ftatefmen or writers, and though they may have purfued the fame mind-enflaving fchemes by more artful, and lefs fanguinary methods, they will be ranked among the Bonners and the Gardiners of paft ages. They muft have been worfe than Bonners and Gardiners, who could purfue the fame ends by the fame means, in this more humane and more enlightened age.

This feems to be the time, when the minds of men are opening to large and generous views of things. Politics are more extended in practice, and better underftood in theory. Religious knowledge is greatly advanced, and the principle of *univerfal toleration* is gaining ground apace. Schemes of ecclefiaftical

policy,

policy, which, in times of barbarity, ignorance, and fuperftition, were intimately interwoven with fchemes of civil policy, and which, in fact, made the greateft part of the old political mixed conftitution, have been gradually excluded; till, at prefent, though ecclefiaftical power be looked upon as an ufeful fupport and auxiliary of civil government, it is pretty much detached from it. And the more fenfible part of mankind are evidently in a progrefs to the belief, that ecclefiaftical and civil jurifdiction, being things of a totally different nature, ought, if poffible, to be wholly difengaged from one another. Religious fentiments, with refpect to their influence on civil fociety, will perhaps be regarded, in time, as a theory of morals, only of a higher and more perfect kind, excellent to enforce a regard to magiftracy, and the political duties, but improperly adopted into the fame fyftem and enforced by the fame penalties. Till we know whether this work, which feems

to

to be going forward in feveral parts of Europe, be of God, or not, let us not take, at leaft any rigid and violent methods to oppofe it, but patiently wait the iffue ; unlefs, in the mean time, the diforders of the ftate abfolutely force us into violent meafures. At prefent, notwithftanding fome trifling alarm, perhaps artfully raifed and propagated, may feem to give a handle to the friends of arbitrary power to make ufe of fome degree of coercion, more gentle meafures feem better adapted to enfure tranquility.

England hath hitherto taken the lead in almoft every thing great and good, and her citizens ftand foremoft in the annals of fame, as having fhaken off the fetters which hung upon the human mind, and called it forth to the exertion of its nobleft powers. And her conftitution has been fo far from receiving any injury from the efforts of thefe her free born enterprifing fons, that fhe is,

in

in part, indebted to them for the unrivalled reputation she now enjoys, of having the beft fyftem of policy in Europe.
After weathering fo many real ftorms,
let us not quit the helm at the apprehenfion of imaginary dangers, but ftea-
dily hold on in what, I truft, is the moft
glorious courfe that a human government can be in. Let all the friends of
liberty and human nature join to free
the minds of men from the fhackles of
narrow and impolitic laws. Let us be
free ourfelves, and leave the bleffings of
freedom to our pofterity.

F I N I S.

For EU product safety concerns, contact us at Calle de José Abascal, 56–1º, 28003 Madrid, Spain or eugpsr@cambridge.org.

www.ingramcontent.com/pod-product-compliance
Ingram Content Group UK Ltd.
Pitfield, Milton Keynes, MK11 3LW, UK
UKHW012345130625
459647UK00009B/540